Garratts & Kalaharis of the Welsh Highland Railway

David Payling

Revised Edition

Festiniog Railway Company

Garratts & Kalaharis of the Welsh Highland Railway

Revised Edition 2022
ISBN 978 0901848 26 0

Published by The Ffestiniog Railway
Harbour Station
Porthmadog LL49 9NF

Designed and Printed by
Gwasg Eryri - Snowdonia Press
Unit 3, Ystad Ddiwydiannol Penamser
Porthmadog LL49 9NZ

2022

Front Cover: *With Cwellyn and the flanks of Mynydd Mawr in the background, newly restored No. 130 pilots No. 87 at Clogwin y Gwin on 27 May 2021.* (David Thurlow)

Back Cover: *No. 87 near Rhyd Ddu with a goods train operated during a photographic charter on 4 November 2021. In the left-hand background are the Glan yr afon quarry tips.* (Chris Parry)

CONTENTS

- I -
FOREWORD

The origins of this book are in the wish to create a history of the ex-South African Railway's narrow gauge Class NG15 locomotives. Sales of the book would assist financially in the current programme to restore one of these engines, No.134, for service on the Welsh Highland Railway. However, when the historical background of the engines began to come together it was realised that the NG15s and also the WHR's other locomotives, the Garratts, plus all the ex-SAR rolling stock, bogies and track had also brought their own history and heritage from the Southern Hemisphere to North Wales.

In the late 1990s our efforts to restore these ex-SAR locomotives to working condition had led to the need to discover the original engineering drawings. There are some 200-250 drawings to assist the engineers and fitters in the construction of each engine class. Approximately 60 of these relate to the boiler alone and, during their service life in South Africa and Namibia, the boilers had been exchanged and randomised to a major extent, complicating the search. The short-lived Transnet Heritage Library proved a fertile source of this material and Boston Lodge now has some 1200 of these drawings available for reference by the engineers and fitters. They were obtained just in time as the facilities for railway information and preservation have shrunk dramatically in South Africa during the last ten years. Even the Heritage Library was closed, just weeks after our locating the drawings for WHR Garratt locomotive No.87.

Since the purchase of equipment through the good offices of the Alfred County Railway in the early 1990s, many useful contacts have been made and good friends found in South Africa. All this has been of great help in the rebuilding of the Welsh Highland Railway. An example of such help was the discovery of the drawings for the narrow gauge rail base plates by the Transnet Railway authorities in Pretoria. This made it possible for us to cast the many thousands of new base plates required for the WHR's new track. It is difficult to think where else in the world we could have found such a source of powerful and modern locomotives and equipment and also to have been able to purchase them on an affordable basis. We owe a debt of gratitude to all concerned.

- II -
Introduction to Revised Edition

Published in a small print run in 2012, this book has been out of print for several years while demand for it has remained constant. In returning it to the market the opportunity has been taken to revise and update the original text where required, particularly with reference to the restoration and entry into service of No 130 and the transfer of K1 to the Statfold Barn Railway in Staffordshire. A number of photographs have been added to expand the locomotives' Welsh stories. The bulk of the book, however, remains the work of David Payling.

The contribution to this book made by Snowdonia Press is acknowledged and appreciated with extreme gratitude.

Peter Johnson
Editor

Herbert William Garratt (1864-1913), who designed most of the locomotives that feature in this book, is buried in Richmond Cemetery. His estate was valued at £3,314 11s 2d
(Keith Holland)

- III -
David Payling

Sadly, the author of this book, David Payling, died on 8 April 2020, aged 79.

Born in Harrow, his parents were teachers. Marrying Maureen Hart in 1967, they had two sons, Richard and Robert. Professionally he was a chemist, working for more than thirty years in research and development and retiring as director of physical chemistry and drug metabolism at Astra Zeneca's Loughborough, Leicestershire, site.

Always a railway enthusiast with a particular interest in narrow gauge lines, he volunteered on the Ffestiniog, Statfold Barn and Welsh Highland Railways. An avid reader and collector of books, he once placed an advertisement seeking to acquire a copy of the out-of-print and then difficult-to-get-hold-of *Narrow Gauge Railways to Portmadoc* by J.I.C. Boyd and was surprised to receive an offer from the author, although he was unable to complete a transaction with him. When his physical health declined in recent years, he donated his railway books to the Ffestiniog Railway Society, to be sold for the benefit of the railway.

David's entrée to authorship came when he was no longer able to be an active volunteer but still wished to contribute. Always cheerful and good company, his books will remain as memorials to his enthusiasm for Welsh narrow gauge railways.

- IV -
Introduction

Visitors to the Welsh Highland Railway are indeed fortunate in the amount of its heritage which has survived the demolition of the railway some 70 years ago. One of the railway's original steam locomotives, Hunslet 2-6-2T *Russell* (1906), has survived into preservation and can be seen today on the Welsh Highland Heritage Railway. Sadly, two of the original locomotives, the War Department Baldwin 4-6-0T "590" and the single Fairlie 0-6-4T *Moel Tryfan* did not survive, having been scrapped during the years after the closure of the railway. However, a War Department Baldwin 4-6-0T of the same type as "590" is now on long term loan at the WHHR and is currently under restoration for service on its line at Porthmadog. A second such locomotive has already been restored to action on the Leighton Buzzard Railway and has appeared as a guest locomotive at the WHHR. It is to be hoped that these engines will be seen hauling trains of heritage passenger carriages on a regular basis on the Welsh Highland Railway.

Locomotives of the original type and power output would be quite unsuitable for the longer, heavier trains on today's rebuilt line. In the 1930s one to three carriages were often sufficient for the traffic available whilst 9-10 cars of today's heavier carriages are commonly required. Indeed one of the factors which had led to the failure of the old company in 1936 had been the performance of its motive power. The engines had proved to be underpowered and, with the poor fuel available to the railway, were frequently unable to keep trains running to time. The scale of the challenge can be seen in the accompanying map and gradient profile

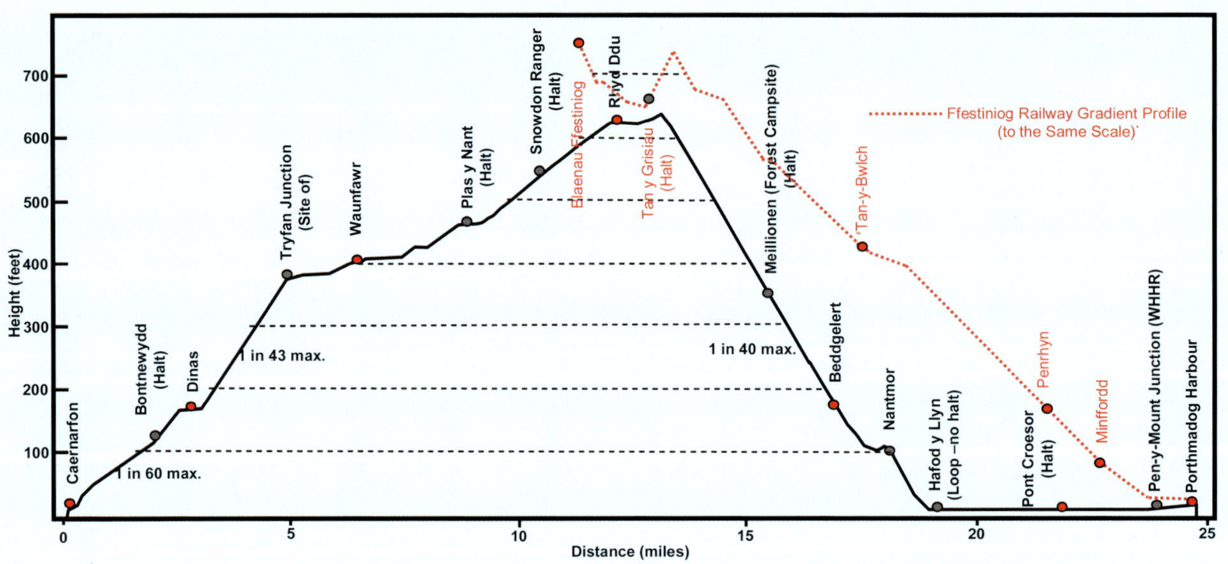

Comparison of Welsh Highland and Ffestiniog Railway Gradient Profiles (David Payling)

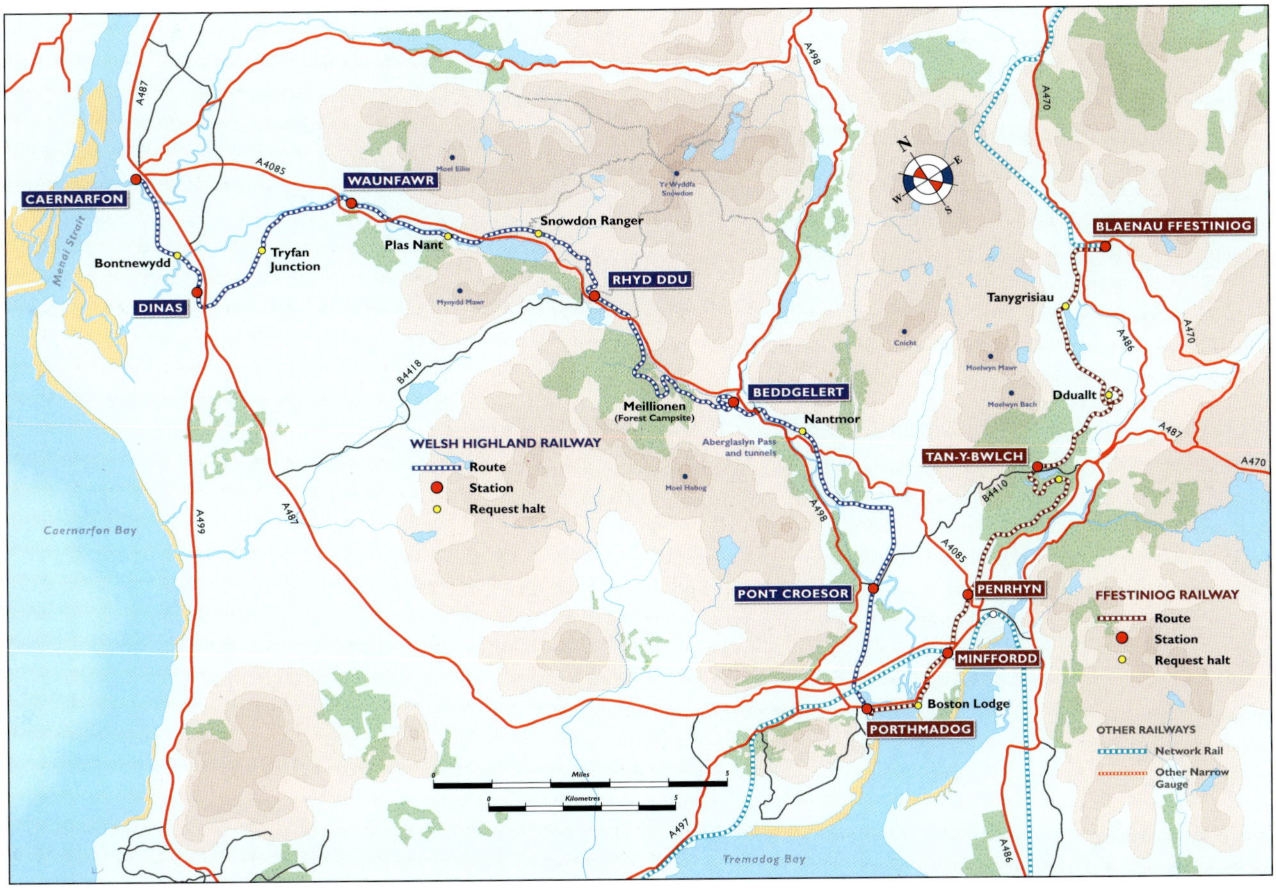

of the Ffestiniog and Welsh Highland Railways. The map shows that both were constrained by the terrain to include sharp curvature. On the former railway the line near Tan-y-Bwlch especially shows this. The WHR follows a tortuous course between Beddgelert and the summit near Pitt's Head with two double horseshoe shaped curves to allow the line to climb the Afon Colwyn valley whilst maintaining a manageable gradient. The gradient profile however shows how much the railways differ. The Ffestiniog has a smoothly graded line with an average gradient of approximately 1 in 80 for much of its original route. The WHR however is constrained at its northern end to accept a gradient of 1 in 40 simply to climb from Dinas to the foot of the quarry inclines at the terminus of its Bryngwyn branch. Likewise the line between the Glaslyn flood plain at Hafod-y-Llyn and the summit near Pitt's Head is similarly constrained by the geography of the district to an almost continuous gradient of 1 in 40. The gradient of this climb of five or more miles is comparable with the two miles long Lickey incline on the southern approach to Birmingham on the British main line network. Here, it had been common in steam days to add a banking engine to help trains up the gradient!

The leaders of the project to restore the WHR were thus very aware of the need for powerful motive power to haul today's heavier trains economically and to an acceptable journey time. The locomotives assembled to meet this challenge in fact bring with them a history and heritage of their own. Curiously, all of them had been designed and built in Britain and Europe during the 20th century for service in the Southern hemisphere. At that time narrow gauge railways represented a potential solution to the question of how to open up transport links in difficult terrain in the developing mining and agricultural economies of Tasmania, German South West Africa (Namibia, since independence from South Africa in 1990) and South Africa.

The oldest of the newcomers to the WHR is the Garratt locomotive, K1, which had been built in 1909 for service in Tasmania. Together with its sister K2, they were the very first locomotives to be built to Herbert Garratt's newly granted patent at the Gorton Foundry of Beyer, Peacock Ltd in Manchester. Likewise No.143, one of the WHR's NG/G16 locomotives, built originally for Southern Africa, was the last Beyer-Garratt and, indeed, the last steam locomotive, to be built by Beyer, Peacock at Gorton in Manchester. So, first and last, the beginnings and the endings of the building of the Garratt locomotive can be seen in North Wales in service today. Even the Kalahari 2-8-2 locomotives built for the Otavi Railway in South West Africa have their own heritage. Historically they represent the culmination of steam locomotive design for a 356 miles long railway of two-foot gauge. Their haulage capacity and capability for fast, free-running have long been regarded by many observers as quite outstanding.

This assembly of motive power on today's WHR has come about through a very happy series of circumstances and opportunities. The availability of the pioneer Garratt, K1, came about through its rescue in 1947 from storage in Tasmania for preservation by its builder, Beyer Peacock, in Manchester. In 1966 this historic locomotive was offered to the Festiniog Railway Society for a nominal sum because Beyer, Peacock was in the process of closing down its Gorton workshops. Fortunately the foresight of the Ffestiniog led to the purchase of the locomotive and it was then displayed for two years at Porthmadog Harbour Station. However there was little prospect of the railway being able to make practical use of the locomotive because it was both too tall and too wide to be readily adapted to the structure gauge of the railway. It was eventually placed on long term loan to the National Railway Museum at York in 1976 where it was displayed in a cosmetically restored condition on one of the turntables. With the initiation of the project to rebuild the WHR the locomotive was recovered from York. Members of the Welsh Highland Railway Society formed the K1 Group and began the process of restoration in 1995.

During the late 1980s, a window of opportunity for the purchase of surplus narrow gauge equipment opened in South Africa. Until that decade the South African Railway network had been strongly (and expensively) supported by government. In particular there were laws in force to limit the extent of road competition for freight traffic. As a result little surplus SAR equipment had ever been available for purchase or preservation. As the 1980s progressed this benign regime was replaced by one (South African Transport Services) which was more friendly to road transport. The result was that the five public narrow gauge railways went into steep decline. By 1990 three of the four lines in Natal had already been closed. Only the 56 mile line from Port Shepstone to Harding had survived. This line had escaped closure only through privatisation as the Alfred County Railway, services recommencing over the whole line on 30th March 1988. However, the ACR replaced steam by diesel haulage for its main traffic of timber in the early 1990s. It retained a small number of operational steam locomotives mainly for its Banana Express tourist passenger operation. Meanwhile at Port Elizabeth in the Eastern Cape the 177 miles long Avontuur Railway had been progressively dieselised since 1973. By the mid-1990s the only steam haulage to remain was the tourist passenger Apple Express. This occasional traffic provided work for only two or three steam locomotives. As a result there were approximately eighteen NG15 2-8-2 locomotives and over thirty Garratt locomotives of two-foot gauge standing out of use in Natal and at Port Elizabeth.

During this period several steam locomotives and other rolling stock were sold to purchasers both inside and outside South Africa. The late Alan Clarke had a senior position in South Africa's Transnet Heritage Foundation. His responsibilities included the organisation of heritage facilities such as a railway museum. The plan was to use proceeds from the sale of surplus rolling stock including locomotives to fund both a museum and the operation of a steam service on the Patensie branch of the Port Elizabeth to Avontuur line. Sadly, this was curtailed by his untimely death and by the turn of the century this window of opportunity was firmly shut. Various organisations in the country had made vociferous protests against the movement of narrow gauge equipment abroad. As a consequence, since the late 1990s, very little narrow gauge rolling stock has left South Africa for preservation. Since then, services have ceased on the two remaining ex-SAR narrow gauge lines. As a consequence, unfortunately, huge amounts of rolling stock and equipment have been scrapped and much that remains faces an uncertain future.

In retrospect it seems a remarkable and fortunate coincidence that, in the early 1990s, relatively modern equipment became available at affordable prices. This was at just the same time as the rebirth of the WHR. With help from a number of sources, including the Alfred County Railway, it became possible to assemble a fleet of powerful locomotives, together with other rolling stock and equipment. Even the excellent ride quality of the WHR's newly built carriages owes much to their ex-SAR bogies.

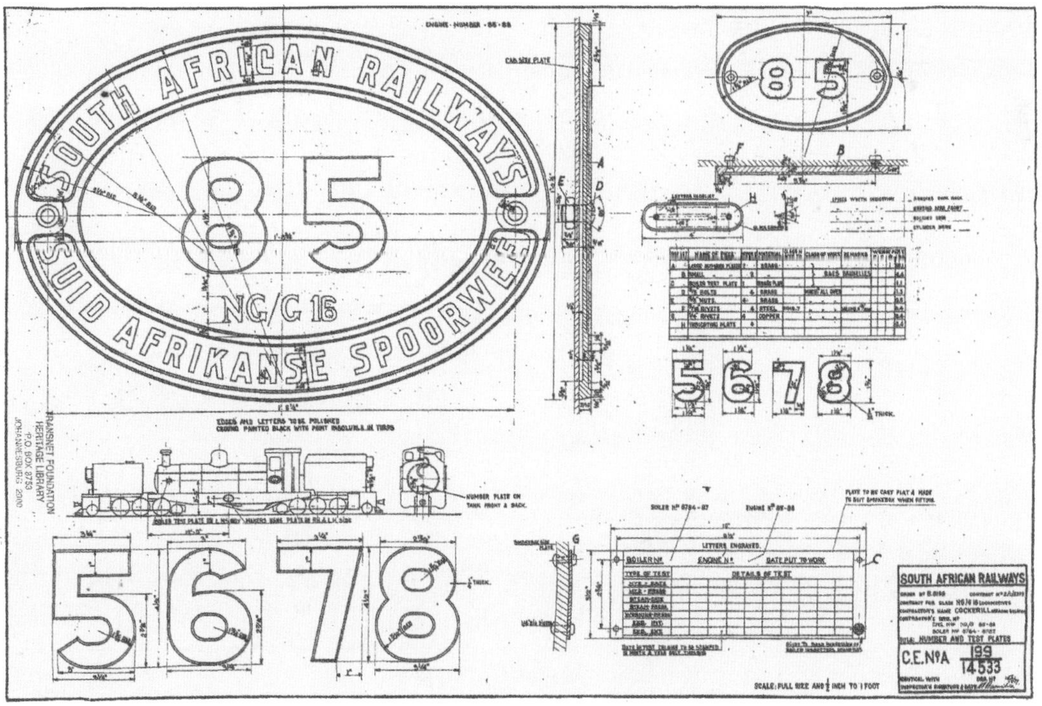

- V -
Development of the Narrow Gauge Garratt Locomotive

The origins of articulated locomotive design lie quite early in railway history. A conventional locomotive is limited in the curvature it can follow by the length of its fixed wheel base. However the development of more powerful steam locomotives requires the use of a larger and hence heavier boiler. This in turn requires the number of supporting wheels and the length of the chassis to be increased so as to prevent the weight on each axle from becoming unacceptable. The longer the fixed wheelbase becomes, the larger becomes the minimum radius of track curvature which the locomotive can follow. Where a railway is constructed with the aim of bringing affordable transport to a difficult terrain the narrow gauge gives the advantage that earthworks could be constructed more lightly and cheaply because a narrow gauge railway can follow the curvature of the contours of the land more easily than one with a broader gauge. The use of articulation to subdivide the fixed wheelbase of a locomotive has long been seen as an attractive way therefore to give the opportunity to operate more powerful locomotives. In more recent times diesel and electric locomotives generally employ power bogies beneath the body which have exactly this effect.

Robert Fairlie was an early advocate of articulation of locomotives. The Ffestiniog Railway was swift to exploit this approach by its support for his concept of a double bogie locomotive. The *Little Wonder*, built to his design for the Ffestiniog Railway in 1869, proved a great success and, over the next fifteen years, another three double Fairlie locomotives were built for the railway. The two independent bogies were powered by a large boiler running the full length of the locomotive. This

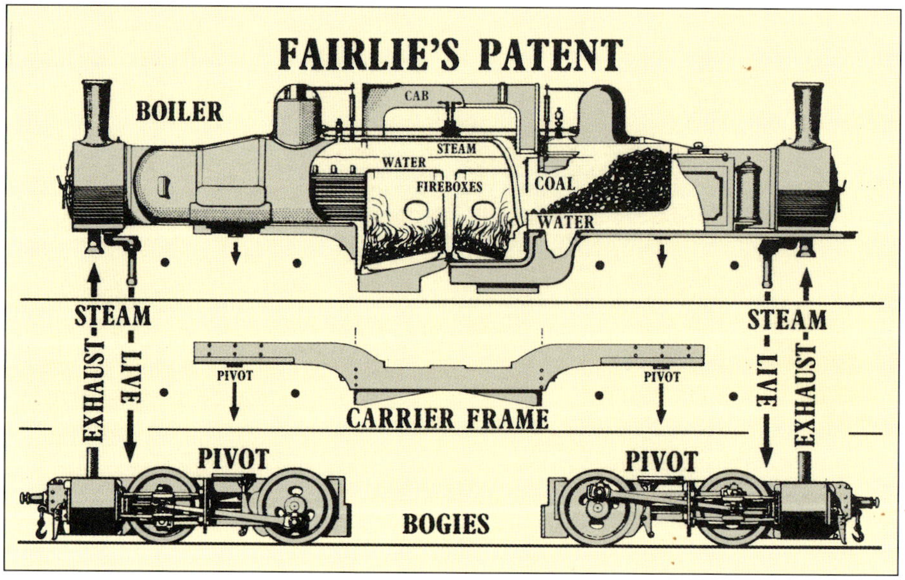

This exploded diagram of the double Fairlie locomotive shows the four basic parts of the locomotive: the boiler and fire box unit, the cradle frame in which they sit and the two power bogies.
(Michael Seymour, FR Archive)

arrangement allowed the locomotive to follow track with much tighter curvature than would be possible for the same number of wheels in a fixed chassis arrangement. The driving cab had to be positioned at the mid point of the locomotive with the driver on one side of the boiler and the fireman on the other, a very restrictive arrangement. The fireman fed twin fireboxes with fire doors opening to his side of the cab whilst the boiler tubes led separately from each firebox to a smoke box and chimney at each end of the locomotive. In mid to late Victorian times many Fairlie locomotives were built for railways all over the world. On the Ffestiniog Railway a double Fairlie could do the work of two of the smaller conventional locomotives, whilst requiring only a single crew, a great advantage in economy.

By the 1890s, however, alternative approaches to articulation had evolved. One, the Mallet locomotive, had a single conventional boiler and firebox. This allowed a full width locomotive cab with the driver and fireman accommodated together. The chassis was divided into two main parts. The frames of the rear portion, beneath the firebox, were rigidly attached to the boiler whilst the leading part of the chassis, beneath the boiler and smokebox, was pivoted to the rear section and free to move from side to side. Both the front and rear sections carried their own cylinders and valve gear. Live steam from the boiler was fed to the rear high pressure cylinders whilst the exhaust steam from these cylinders was piped via flexible jointing to be re-used to power the front, low pressure bogie. The Mallet was thus usually a compound locomotive, the steam being used successively to drive first the high pressure cylinders and then the low pressure cylinders before reaching the smokebox and chimney.

The articulated locomotive patent issued in 1907 to Herbert W Garratt also called for a single boiler unit and cab. In this case however, the boiler was supported in a cradle frame which was pivoted to a steam bogie at each end. The front bogie supported a water tank whilst the rear bogie supported a bunker with accommodation for both the fuel and a further water space. One of the advantages of the design

The Mallet locomotive, illustrated by Statfold Barn Railway's Jung 0-4 + 4-0TT (4878, 1930), was developed at the end of the 19th century and has a conventional cab and boiler. The high pressure engine chassis is attached rigidly to the boiler unit whilst the leading, low pressure, bogie is pivoted to the high pressure unit. (David Payling)

This 2010 view inside the erecting shop at Statfold Barn, shows part of the frames of Jung Mallet No.4878 during re-assembly. The boiler and cab will form a rigid fixture on the rear (left) chassis frames whilst the heavy vertical upper and lower pivots, visible at its front, will form the connection to the front, low pressure, engine. (David Payling)

was that as the locomotive followed track curvature it occupied space within the curve, rather than projecting outwards beyond the track. This had been a disadvantage of certain of the other articulated locomotive designs which had appeared around the turn of the 20th century. Another advantage was that the boiler cradle gave the maximum of space for a well designed large boiler and firebox without conflict for space with the design of the power bogies. The Mallet design, in contrast, gave no more space for the boiler and firebox than a conventional fixed wheelbase engine.

In 1909 discussions were in progress between Beyer, Peacock and the Tasmanian Government Railways (TGR) for the purchase of new motive power. It was required for the North East Dundas Tramway where traffic growth between the mines at Williamsford and the smelters at Zeehan was outstripping the capacity of the line. The existing motive power included two small Sharp Stewart tank engines and a large, powerful, German-built Hagen locomotive. This machine had a 2-6-4-0T wheel arrangement. The driving wheels were coupled in two groups in a novel way which was intended to allow the locomotive to follow sharp track curvature. This was important on the NE Dundas Tramway because the radius of curvature was as sharp as 99 ft. whilst gradients were as steep as 1 in 27½. In fact the tramway ran some 18 miles to cover a distance of only 10 miles as the crow flies. In contrast our own WHR has track curvature limited officially to a radius of not less than 150 ft with gradients rarely steeper than 1 in 40. Despite its design the Hagen locomotive was proving very punishing to the track of the tramway and the railway authorities were open to suggestions for motive power that would combine strong power output with acceptable wear to the track.

The discussions between TGR and Beyer, Peacock led to an order for the construction of the first two locomotives ever to be built to HW Garratt's patent. These pioneer locomotives were completed at Gorton in 1909 as TGR's K1 and K2. Although Beyer, Peacock initially had offered a simple expansion locomotive design the TGR had insisted upon compound expansion. The reasons for this are unclear although, in the early 20th century, perhaps the most favoured articulated locomotive design had become the Mallet. These locomotives were generally built with compound steam expansion, perhaps causing the expectation that an articulated engine with four cylinders should be a compound? To comply with this the cylinders of K1 and K2 were positioned at the inboard end of the power bogies. This allowed the shortest possible distance for exhaust steam to travel from the high pressure cylinders of the rear bogie to the low pressure cylinders of the leading bogie so as to minimise condensation.

The two new locomotives proved to be a great success on the NE Dundas Tramway. Despite this, the use of compound expansion was not repeated on future Garratt designs. Although approximately 1650 Garratt locomotives were constructed by various builders between 1909 and 1968, almost all were simple expansion engines rather than compounds. In most cases the cylinders were positioned at the outer ends of the bogies where they could best balance the weight of the boiler unit.

The three main parts of the Garratt locomotive are illustrated by this exploded diagram of Tasmanian Garratt, K1. It consists of a boiler and cab unit sitting within a cradle frame, pivoted to the leading and trailing power bogies. (Leith Paxton)

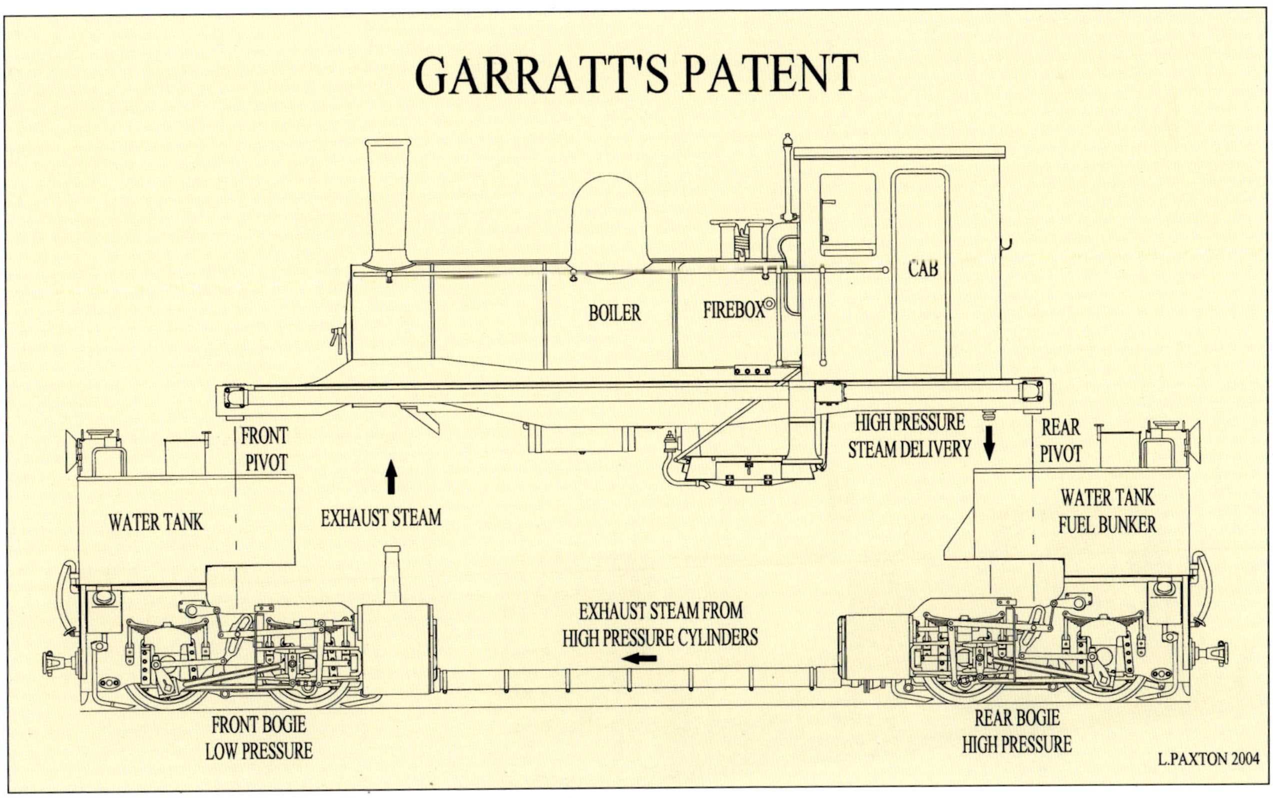

- VI -
Evolution of the NG/G16 Beyer-Garratts

In the early years of the 20th century the South African Railway's authorities were seeking motive power for their 24 in. narrow gauge lines in Natal and in the Cape. At the Union in 1910 they had inherited a selection of modest sized locomotives from the Cape and the Natal Government Railways. The challenge was to find a locomotive type with adequate power for future traffic needs combined with the ability to follow the tight curvature of these railways (the minimum curve radius was 150 ft.). They became aware of Beyer, Peacock's new Garratt patent locomotive designs and, in 1914, placed an order for three narrow gauge engines. They became South African Railways Class NG/G11 and were eventually delivered in 1919-20, construction and delivery having been delayed by the First World War.

For the 24 in. gauge the NG/G11s were large locomotives with a 19.5 sq. ft. grate and a saturated steam boiler with a Belpaire firebox. They had a 2-6-0 + 0-6-2 wheel arrangement, the bogies being constructed with plate frames. The engines were subjected to trials on the Umzinto to Donnybrook line (the Stuartstown Branch) in Natal and won very favourable opinions. In his Operations Report for 1921-1922 the SAR's General Manager wrote: "The narrow gauge Garratt engines placed in service on the Stuartstown Branch are most economical and have reduced train mileage and trainmen's hours. Their introduction has also effected a saving of one engine and one engine crew." A follow-up order was placed for two more NG/G11 locomotives. They were delivered in 1925, although to an improved specification including a superheated boiler and piston valves for the cylinders. The scene was now set for a future for the South African narrow gauge based upon articulated Garratt motive power.

One further refinement of the specification for SAR Garratt locomotives that emerged from the trials of the new engines was the inclusion of inner carrying axles on each bogie, Bissell trucks. Beyer, Peacock's fitter, who had supervised the erection of the engines and their trials on arrival in South Africa, observed the sideways movement of the inner ends of the bogies from a perch beneath the locomotive. From this uncomfortable position on one of the Cape Gauge engines he could see considerable sideways oscillation. This was addressed in most future builds by the inclusion of inner trucks with side control.

NG/G11 No.51 (BP 5975, 1920) was the first Garratt to be delivered for use on the South African narrow gauge. Note the Belpaire firebox, plate frame bogies and slide valves. (Beyer Peacock, Transnet Heritage Library)

The pioneer Hanomag NG/G13 was No.58 (10549, 1927). The works photograph shows the inner and outer carrying axles and a round top firebox. Some 83 years after this photo was taken the boiler (No.7850) was still in service, carried by No.87 on the WHR. (Hanomag, N Fields Collection)

~ 1. Hanomag NG/G13 (1927, 1928) Nos.58 - 60, Nos.49, 50 & Nos.77-83 ~

The expiry of the Garratt patent in 1927 freed SAR from the tie to Beyer, Peacock in Manchester. It was now possible to look more widely for a supplier for the next generation of narrow gauge Garratts. In Hannoversche Maschinenbau-AG, known as Hanomag, SAR found an eager new partner. The *Hanomag Nachrichten* (Hanomag's House magazine) for November 1927 records the initiation, by Colonel Collins (CME of SAR), of a "permanent collaboration between Hanomag and SAR." Its first fruits were 40 Garratt locomotives including 37 of type GF for secondary duties on the Cape gauge and three NG/G13 Garratts for the narrow gauge. The locomotives were described as being "from a scheme or project of Col. Collins, worked out and built" by Hanomag.

The new German/South African designs proved to be a great success, the GFs lasting for many years in service and being built in further batches. On the narrow gauge the first three NG/G13s (Nos.58 - 60) were sent to Natal and proved to be free steaming and powerful. An extension of the order was placed immediately for two more locomotives (Nos.49, 50) which were delivered in 1928, eventually also being allocated to the Natal lines. A further order added another seven engines (Nos.77-83), all of which were delivered to Port Elizabeth in 1928 for the Avontuur Branch.

The NG/G13s were a radical re-think of the narrow gauge Garratt design. The boiler and Belpaire firebox of the NG/G11 was discarded in favour of a round topped firebox and a short, broad boiler with a fifteen element superheater. This arrangement took full advantage of Garratt's principle of achieving boiler efficiency through the use of a short, wide boiler together with a wide firebox. A rocking grate was specified. Although the grate (19.2 sq. ft.) of the new design was actually slightly smaller than the NG/G11, the steaming was transformed. The NG/G13 proved to be a locomotive rarely short of steam.

The power bogies were radically redesigned on the basis of outside bar frames rather than plate frames. The generous cylinders and piston valves were controlled by Walschaert's valve gear. The chassis was based on a 2-6-2 + 2-6-2 wheel arrangement, inner carrying axles being included, unlike the NG/G11s, to give the engine greater stability whilst running. The coupled axles carried fly cranks and weights, the driving axle being the inner axle to allow the longest possible connecting rod. The outer carrying axles were conventional Bissell trucks and carried almost as much weight as the coupled axles (approximately 6¼ tons). However the inner carrying axle was built to the Golsdorf principle where a conventional fixed axle is allowed to follow curved track more easily by provision for a small amount of lateral movement. The suspension of all axles was compensated by beams bearing on the axleboxes. This gave the advantage to SAR management that the locomotives could be operated safely on light track, 48lb. per yard rail being sufficient. There was, however, a price to pay for this even weight distribution in that the outer and inner trucks caused a significant reduction in adhesive weight. The earlier design of the double Fairlie, by contrast, had no carrying axles and thus enjoyed 100% adhesive weight.

The "permanent collaboration" between Hanomag and SAR was destined to be far shorter than had been hoped as the Hanomag locomotive construction business was sold to Henschel & Sohn GmbH in 1931. Although the locomotives were judged a great success, there were drawbacks. The bogie units were too stiff, possibly because the inner Golsdorf axle allowed the wheelset a sideways movement of only $^{31}/_{32}$ in. As a result the locomotives proved prone to cracking of the main frames between the inner carrying axle and the adjacent driving axle. The sanding arrangements appeared to be something of an afterthought! They were based on gravity feed from sand boxes placed here and there around the locomotive including a box beneath the driver's seat, together with boxes set into the inner corners of the bunker and front water tank. The NG/G13s were prone to slipping in adverse rail conditions, partly due to a lack of reliability of the sanding arrangements and partly to the adhesive weight (65%) which was reduced significantly by the two carrying axles on each bogie. Correction of a wheel slip by closing the steam regulator unfortunately cut off steam to both bogies. In this sense the older double Fairlie locomotive design had a second advantage in that the driver had a separate regulator control for each bogie, allowing superior control of slipping. The NG/G13 cabs were very small and proved to be very hot for the footplate crew in South African conditions. This was aggravated by the heat of the steam fittings which were located inside or very close to the cab. The live steam manifold was set against the cab spectacle plate, whilst the vacuum ejector and the sight feed lubricators and their steam supplies were both located inside the cab, altogether making for a very hot working

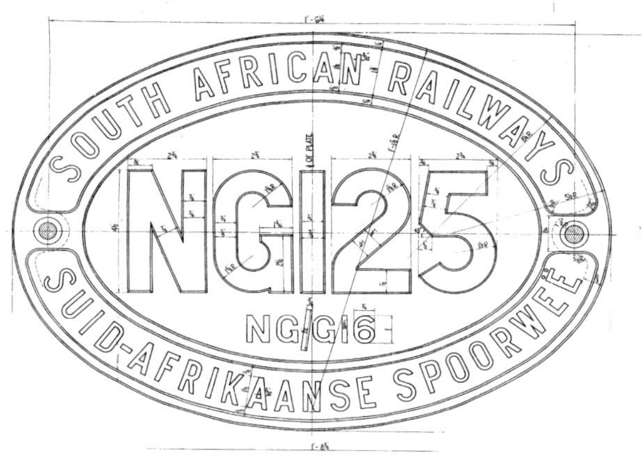

~ 2. John Cockerill NG/G16 (1936) Nos.85 - 88 ~

By 1936 SAR required more narrow gauge Garratts. This time, however, the contract went to Beyer, Peacock although the railway authorities made it clear that they wanted locomotives which would include the most successful features of the NG/G13s, as designed by Hanomag. The Gorton workshops were very busy at the time. The Beyer-Garratt Locomotive catalogue (published by Beyer, Peacock in 1947) records that the building of the four locomotives for SAR was carried out "to our design under license arrangement by John Cockerill of Seraing, Belgium." However, the *Railway Gazette* of August 1935 recorded that the order had been for four NG/G13s! Neither source mentions Hanomag, or that company's role in the origins of the design. The four were delivered to Durban in the Spring of 1937 and allocated to Umzinto (Nos.85 and 86) and Port Shepstone (Nos.87 and 88). Under magnification the Cockerill works photograph shows the original classification as Class NG/G13 which can be seen on the cab-side number plate. These plates were replaced later by new ones carrying the NG/G16 identity. Most of the pre-war Garratts carried brass cab-side plates which showed the running number centrally placed but, unlike most post-war engines (except for the 1957 Henschel NG15s), with no "NG" prefix.

The cab-side number plate fitted to No.86 when new, declared it to be a NG/G13! The plate was later exchanged for one identifying the locomotive as a NG/G16. (Transnet Heritage Library)

To the eye there was little difference in the appearance of the new NG/G16s from the 1927-8 NG/G13s. The boiler and cradle were essentially unchanged although the boiler water feed to the clack boxes in front of the dome was now carried via polished copper pipes sloping diagonally from below the running board up to the clack boxes just in front of the dome. One change was the lighting where electricity replaced the paraffin lamps of the NG/G13s. Thus the boiler mountings included a steam turbine electricity generator, to the rear of the dome, to supply the cab lights and large American Pyle headlights on the tank and bunker ends. The cab, with its cramped and hot conditions for the crew, went largely unchanged. An attempt was made to address the sanding problem by the placement of a

The works photograph shows No.86, second engine of the first batch of NG/G16s, built by John Cockerill of Seraing, Belgium. Note the remarkable steam operated sand box mounted on the front water tank, adjacent to the tank filler cap. (Transnet Heritage Library)

diamond shaped sand box on top of the front water tank, adjacent to the filler flap. It must have been difficult to keep the sand dry! The chassis problems were addressed to allow adequate side movement to follow curved track, avoiding frame cracking. This was achieved by exchanging the Golsdorf axles for normal Bissell trucks with full compensation. The truck axles were also equipped with Timken roller bearings although the weight distribution between the axles was unchanged, leaving a heavy load on the outer trucks.

In the new roller bearing design the outer truck continued to require very strong side control springing. The new arrangement of the outer Bissell truck caused its frame mounted leaf spring to share some of the sideways motion of the truck through chain links from the spring hangers to the axlebox. Unfortunately this sideways movement caused a twisting force on the leaf springs. This in turn led to a tendency to fractures of the leaves at the spring buckle. The problem was never completely resolved in SAR days despite modifications to the chain connections and to the number of spring leaves, etc.

~ 3. Beyer, Peacock NG/G16 (1939) Nos.109 - 116 ~

A batch of eight more NG/G16s was delivered by Beyer, Peacock in 1939 (Nos.109 - 116). With this batch the Garratts on the SAR narrow gauge, by 1939, totalled some 32 locomotives. They were the initial five NG/G11s, 12 NG/G13s, 12 NG/G16s and three smaller locomotives (Classes NG/G12 from Anglo-Franco-Belge and NG/G14 from Hanomag) for lines with a very restricted axle loading.

Changes to the NG/G16 design from the John Cockerill locomotives (1936) included a slight lengthening of the cab towards the rear (five inches!) which allowed the inclusion of a narrow side window to the rear of the doorway. No modifications to the boiler mountings were made however to relieve the very hot conditions in the cab. There were also minor modifications which had little effect on the appearance of the locomotives. They required the issue of an additional 96 replacement or supplementary drawings against the original 203 issued in 1936 (121 drawings from 1936 were used again).

The second batch of NG/G16s was built by Beyer, Peacock at Gorton in 1939. The photograph of No.115 shows that some thought had been given to crew comfort by the enlarging of the cab by five inches to the rear, including a window to the rear of the doorway. (Transnet Heritage Library)

~ 4. Beyer, Peacock NG/G16 (1950) Nos.125 - 131 ~

After the Second World War a batch of seven locomotives was built by Beyer, Peacock in 1950 (Nos.125 - 131). The opportunity was now taken to update the NG/G16 design. The pre-war drawings were replaced by a completely new set of 217 drawings.

There were many significant changes to the locomotives from the pre-war batches. The earlier inadequate sanding arrangements were replaced by cast sand boxes attached to the front of the water tank and the rear of the bunker. Gravity feed of the sand was retained however.

The comfort of the crew was at last addressed by the moving of as many as possible of the hot steam fittings to the outside of the cab. For example the sight feed lubricators were replaced by Wakefield type 7Z mechanical lubricators on the buffer beams at each end of the locomotive. The vacuum ejector was moved out to the side of the firebox on the driver's side and the steam manifold was moved away from the cab spectacle plate, the twin Ross pop safety valves being re-positioned side by side at the front of the firebox top to make space available. Another small change was to the whistle mounting and the top feed clack boxes in front of the dome. These now exchanged places locating the whistle close to the dome. The steam turbine generator was moved from the boiler top to the LHS footplate, powering Stone's Tonum headlights on the tank and bunker ends. On the bogies a small change was made to the springing of the outer trucks. On earlier batches the axle boxes were attached to their spring ends by chain links. On the 1950 locomotives the chains were replaced by "flexible links." This change was repeated in the two final batches. The bogie pivots were updated to a patented design which included wedge adjustment and mechanical lubrication.

The first post-war batch of NG/G16s was completed at Gorton in 1950. Significant changes included improvement of crew comfort by moving the steam manifold forward away from the cab and replacement of the hot sight feed lubricator in the cab with buffer beam mounted mechanical lubricators. The vacuum brake exhauster was moved out to the firebox side. Sand boxes were now attached to the ends of the water tank and bunker. (Transnet Heritage Library)

~ 5. Beyer, Peacock NG/G16 (1958) Nos.137 - 143 ~

A further batch of seven locomotives was built by Beyer, Peacock in 1958. The order was placed by agents for the Tsumeb Mining Corporation of South West Africa, working closely with SAR to ensure adequate motive power on the 600mm gauge Otavi Branch (256 miles) in SWA. The agreement between Tsumeb Corporation and SAR was that, for budgetary reasons, the Corporation would order the locomotives although they would be operated as though they were SAR property. The agreement included provision for the guaranteed resale of the seven to SAR to be put into service elsewhere on the SAR narrow gauge when the planned gauge conversion of the Otavi branch was eventually complete. As built, the locomotives carried Tsumeb Corporation running numbers (TC6 - TC12). However the re-gauging of the Otavi Branch to the Cape Gauge was completed early, the last narrow gauge trains running in November 1960. As a result the seven locomotives were shipped instead to South Africa, their running numbers eventually becoming Nos.137 - 143.

The 1950 drawings were used in part (64 of them) although supplemented by a new set of 195 drawings. Changes to the locomotives from the 1950 batch were essentially to suit them to the long length of the Otavi Railway and the infrequent staging points for water or fuel.

For the first time in the NG/G16 series welded construction was used for both the front tank and rear bunker. The cut outs at the inner lower corners of tank and bunker were more prominent than on the 1950 engines and no longer used as space for sand boxes. The front tank was given a marginally taller height (½ in!), a flat top and an extra three inches width, bringing its capacity up to 1325 gallons. The rear bunker was built with no water space and could hold 6tons 4cwt of coal. Its length was 10½ in. shorter than previous builds but 2⅛ in. taller. The difference visually between this bunker and the other NG/G16 builds was that it extended only to the line of the cut out above the cylinders and coasting valves. The front and rear buffer beams carried water pipes and valves, to be used in conjunction with a semi permanently coupled 3200 gallon tank car. Although water tank cars did not come into general use with the NG/G16s, some impression of them can be obtained from Port

The works photo of the 1958 batch of NG/G16s shows No.142 identified as Tsumeb Corporation No.TC11. Note the small Tsumeb ownership plate on the boiler cradle to the rear of the Beyer, Peacock works plate. (Transnet Heritage Library)

Elizabeth's Apple Express Garratt, No.131, which ran through the 1990s until 2005 with such a car. A prominent water tank vent was provided to the rear of the front water tank.

The cab sides were modified on the driver's side (RHS) to give better clearance for the reversing handle, a bulge being built into both the plating and the outside hand rail. On the left a smaller bulge accommodated the hand brake which had been moved from the rear of the cab (earlier batches).

On the boiler top the whistle location moved from the front boiler ring to the top of the steam manifold in front of the cab.

~ 6. Hunslet Taylor NG/G16 (1967 - 8) Nos.149 – 156 ~

A batch of eight locomotives was built by Hunslet Taylor (Johannesburg) in 1967-8 (Nos.149 - 156). The Beyer, Peacock locomotive building business was closing down at the time of the order being placed and they had therefore declined the contract. Eventually Hunslet Taylor was selected and they relied on their parent company in Leeds, UK, to supply the eight boilers and one spare. Many other components were also supplied by UK manufacturers through Hunslet in Leeds. For example the slabs of special steel from which the bar frames of the power bogies were cut and fabricated, were also supplied from a UK source.

By this time SAR engineering drawings were managed and indexed in a new way. It differed from the previous system, all items of a locomotive including valves, washers, etc., however small, now being given a part number within a central stores data base.

Changes from the design of the 1958 locomotives were relatively few, the exceptions being the rear

The boilers for the eight Hunslet Taylor locomotives, plus one spare, were built in 1967 by Hunslet in Leeds. This view shows two under construction. (Andrew Neale Collection)

Below: *The works plate of the final Hunslet Taylor NG/G16 of 1968, No.156.* (Tony Leeson)

bunker and the locomotive's headlights. The rear bunker reverted to the 1950 design and carried both coal (four tons) and water (600 gallons). Welded construction was used and the front (flat top) tank had a 1300 gallon capacity. The large Stone Tonum single bulb headlights fitted to earlier locomotives were replaced by motor car type twin sealed beam halogen headlights, mounted similarly to the earlier pattern. Many of these modifications were extended to older locomotives as they went through the workshops for general repairs. For example the sealed beam headlights gained general use. The attachment of sand boxes to the tank and bunker ends also became more widespread, especially on the NG/G13s working on heavy limestone duties on the steeply graded climb from Loerie towards Port Elizabeth.

Construction of the Hunslet Taylor locomotives brought the Garratt locomotive building history to a close. At its outset in 1927 the NG/G13 design had included forward looking and ground breaking features. Whilst the further development of the Garratt locomotive elsewhere had continued to new levels of innovation the development of the NG/G16 design had been relatively modest over the forty years to 1968. One such lack was the absence of an efficient rail sanding system. This deficiency was never successfully tackled in SAR days although almost every batch of engines had a slightly different sanding arrangement. Another was the bogie suspension where the heavy weight on the outer trucks and inadequate spring mountings led to frequent spring breakages. More positively the SAR authorities had gained the benefit of economies in cost from the interchangeability of parts, especially boilers, through this standardisation.

No works photograph has been discovered for the NG/G16s constructed by Hunslet Taylor of Johannesburg in 1967-8. However, this photograph shows the final locomotive No.156 almost brand new on 9th October 1968 at Port Shepstone running shed. This was the occasion of a visit by members of the Ian Allan/RCTS tour of South Africa that year. (Ralph Wilks)

~ 7. NG/G16A (Girdlestone): Nos.141 (1989) and 155 (1990) ~

With the formation of the Alfred County Railway Co. in 1987, the board of directors was keenly aware of the need to update the basically sixty years old design of the NG/G16 Garratts. This was to ensure their most economical running and servicing so as to be able to compete successfully with the road hauliers for the key traffic in timber. The position of Chief Mechanical Engineer went to Phil Girdlestone who had already amassed considerable experience of modern steam practice through his innovative work on combustion and other aspects of locomotive design. This included the gas producer combustion system applied to the Ffestiniog's *Linda* in the early 1980s followed by similar work at Hugh Philips Engineering in South Wales whilst refurbishing engines for famine relief work in Sudan.

Beyer-Garratt No.141 (1958) was selected as the most suitable for upgrading, this engine having acquired a boiler from one of the 1968 engines at its last workshop repair together with a new steel inner firebox. The locomotive was rebuilt at the workshops at Port Shepstone. Modifications to the firebox were made to incorporate the gas producer combustion system (GPCS). The most serious waste of fuel in the coal fired steam locomotive is coal particle carryover at high grate loadings. The GPCS reduces this loss by gasifying the coal and burning the gas produced in secondary air admitted over the fire bed. This results in the airflow through the fire bed being reduced to 30-50% of the total required in normal combustion at the same rate. A restricted airspace grate was fitted, the majority of the air now being admitted through over-fire inlets

The first gas producer combustion conversion, NG/G16A No.141, stands on shed at Port Shepstone after an intermediate overhaul in May 1990. (Phil Girdlestone)

NG/G16A No.141, stands at the Izingolweni servicing point with a train of mixed goods and containers for Harding on 25th July 1990. (Tony Leeson)

in the firebox sides and through the firebox door. Some exhaust steam was mixed with the primary air. This cooled the fire bed to below the temperature of ash fusion and produced gas for burning in the secondary air streams. Together these changes eliminate clinker formation and greatly reduce the amount of unburned coal lost through the chimney at high rates of working by means of the reduced primary airflow.

The GPCS increases the amount of draught required because of losses incurred by the turbulent mixing requirements in the firebox. To achieve the draught required a Lempor exhaust system, as developed by LD Porta, was installed. Whilst producing the increased draught required, it did so with a nozzle area some 50% greater than the standard engines. The reduced back pressure this gave to exhaust steam naturally translated into increased power output. The Master Mechanics spark arrestor was redesigned to reduce the draught loss across it and smoothed where possible to ease the passage of the gases. The valve gear too was updated with the aim of allowing steam entry and exit from the cylinders more efficiently. Computer calculations were the basis for redesign of the valves to increase the opening of ports at inlet and exhaust at all cut-off settings. Lightweight, streamlined, fully floating, articulated seven ring piston valves were devised to seal better than the original four ring design.

Mechanical lubricators with more feeds were obtained from scrapped Cape gauge GMAM Garratts to give an improved and extended lubrication system. Other improvements included steam operated cylinder drain cocks, an enlarged water filler access, improved lighting for inspection of the motion and a fireman's injector water overflow. The original bunker, with space only for coal, was replaced with one which carried both coal and water. The locomotive was turned out in the same bright red as the SAR's *Red Devil*, soon acquiring the nick-name of the *Red Dragon*.

After tuning up work had been completed, comparative coal consumption trials were carried out with standard Garratt No.116. This engine was chosen because it was in good mechanical condition and steamed well. These tests showed a coal saving of 20% with No.141. However the trials were carried out on the upper part of the line between Harding and Izingolweni which had easier ruling gradients of 1 in 60 as opposed to 1 in 37 on the Port Shepstone - Izingolweni section. This favoured No.116 and penalised No.141 since the required power output (and thus grate loading) was lower and it can be assumed that a 25% overall coal saving was more realistic. In summary the rebuilding had achieved an increased steaming capacity, a greater breathing capacity of the improved valves and exhaust, plus a reduced back pressure in the cylinder exhaust. Together these had yielded a noticeable increase in power output, although at the cost of an increased tendency to wheel slip. The highest power recorded on test was 705 ihp although it was estimated that over 800 ihp was attainable. This was sufficient to allow a decision to convert a second engine, No.155. Meanwhile, further improvements to No.141 included the fitting of roller bearings to the return crank and eccentric rod end assemblies. Availability for service of the newly converted engine was approximately 90% during its first months of work.

Phil Girdlestone died on 20 April 2016, aged 62. His ashes were interred at the Ffestiniog Railway's memorial overlooking Boston Lodge.

The two producer gas combustion locomotives, Nos.141 and 155, head a loaded timber train in 1992. Unusually they are running chimney-first towards Port Shepstone, on the climb between Bongwana and Nquabeni. (Anthony Stanton)

~ 8. NG/G16 GARRATT MAINTENANCE in SOUTH AFRICA ~

In South Africa maintenance of the locomotives was carried out locally under the care of the motive power foreman at Port Elizabeth (Humewood Road) and at the various depots in Natal. This would include routine day to day attention and anything up to and including intermediate repairs to the boiler and chassis.

Main workshop, or general, repairs for the Avontuur Branch locomotives were carried out at Uitenhage (near Port Elizabeth) where there were facilities to carry out all boiler and chassis repairs or rebuilding. The Natal branches at Estcourt, Umlaas Road, Umzinto and Port Shepstone shared the Pietermaritzburg facilities near Durban. Since the railway workshops were not located on the narrow gauge lines it was necessary to devise a way of transporting engines from their home depots. In both the Eastern Cape and Natal the arrangement was to use transporter wagons. These were often ancient Cape gauge flat cars fitted with rails welded to the deck. There were bridging sections between pairs of wagons so that locomotives and other vehicles could straddle more than one car. At the running sheds both at Humewood Road in Port Elizabeth and at Port Shepstone in Natal there were loading bays which allowed an engine to be

Garratt No.127 stands in the roll-on loading dock at Humewood Road on 14th July 1973, loaded on two Cape Gauge transfer wagons. Although this was the starting point for journeys to Uitenhage for workshop repairs, No.127 was in fact departing for its new home on the Umzinto line in Natal. (Neil Mardell, NGRS Archive)

propelled carefully from a narrow gauge siding onto the transporter wagons.

One of the curiosities of the SAR and South West African narrow gauge was that transporter wagons do not seem to have been used to any extent to carry loaded Cape gauge vehicles to or from a narrow gauge destination. The management had been prompted to consider this process early in the 20th century when the SAR authorities commissioned a report from the consultancy of Mr E R Calthrop on a proposed narrow gauge line near Johannesburg. In commenting on the proposal he made the point that a 24 inch gauge transporter would be quite acceptable for Cape gauge vehicles, whilst the wider 2ft 6in gauge would be preferable for standard gauge vehicles.

On completion of each nine yearly General Repair a locomotive would typically leave the workshop with a different boiler from the one it had arrived with. This was the result of pooling the boilers so that on completion of its chassis overhaul a locomotive would take the next available repaired boiler. Since a boiler repair took longer than a chassis overhaul there was considerable swapping of boilers between locomotives. Effectively there were two boiler pools. There was one for the twelve NG/G13s, which were compatible with those of the twelve pre-war NG/G16s. The second pool consisted of boilers for the twenty-two post-war NG/G16s, all of which were interchangeable with each other. The reason for the separation of the pools of pre-war from post-war boilers lay in their fittings.

The pre-war engines had sight feed lubricators and their piping inside the cab and on the boiler side. They also had the vacuum brake ejector mounting inside the cab whilst the steam manifold was placed very close in front of the cab spectacle plate. Boilers of NG/G16s built after the Second World War had no attachments for lubricators, these now being replaced by mechanical lubricators located on the buffer beams at the outer end of the bogies. The vacuum brake ejector was now mounted outside the cab on the right hand side of the firebox. To improve crew comfort the hot steam manifold was placed further from the cab spectacle plate. This in turn required changes to the safety valve flanges, placing the valves side by side rather than in line along the firebox top. Boiler swaps thus took place freely between locomotives from the post-war batches. However swaps between pre-war and post-war locomotives were less common, requiring significant modification of the mountings and fittings. Interestingly this feature of SAR workshop practice has meant that the WHR locomotives carry boilers from almost every batch of NG/G16s and NG/G13s (see Appendix).

- VII -
History of the WHR Garratts
K1

The history of Garratt locomotive K1 is described first as, not only was this the first engine to be built to Herbert Garratt's patent, it was also the first locomotive of this type to arrive on the Ffestiniog and Welsh Highland Railways. In 1909 two locomotives, K1 and K2 were built by Beyer, Peacock to the order of the Tasmanian Government Railways. After inspection at Gorton works they were shipped to their new home at Zeehan in North West Tasmania. For the next twenty years they were to be the principal motive power for the 18 miles long North East Dundas Tramway to Williamsford. They proved to be masters of their work on this difficult railway, hauling both its passenger and goods traffic. Their four wheel bogies proved capable of following the line's tortuous course with ease. By contrast,

In works primer paint K1 undergoes its steam test in the works yard at Beyer Peacock's in 1909.
(K1 Group Collection)

K1 is posed for an official portrait on arrival in Tasmania in 1910.
(K1 Group Collection)

Above: *K1 stands at Zeehan during the 1920s. The massive additional sand box on the water tank top is testimony to the difficulty of working trains over this heavily graded tramway.* (K1 Group Collection)

Right: *The incline to the Hercules Mine rose 1642 ft from the site of the now abandoned NE Dundas Tramway at Williamsford. It was a mile in length with a maximum gradient of 1 in 1.5! The miners have just ended their shift and descended in the incline's man-rider on a day in 1971.* (Peter Ralph)

the earlier Hagen locomotive had proved very punishing to the track, its mechanically complex form of articulation being unequal to the task. It was transferred away to other less demanding duties.

On the NE Dundas Tramway the radius of the sharpest curves was less than 100ft whilst the gradients were as steep as 1 in 25 in places. The switchback nature of the route challenged the power output of locomotives whether they were in charge of trains either towards or away from Zeehan. It is said that new tyres were required for K1 and K2 within four years, a remarkable rate of wear! This, combined with the later fitting of massive additional sand boxes on the tank and bunker tops in place of the original headlamps, gives testimony to the difficult route of the tramway.

According to a contemporary article the locomotives were capable of hauling up to 70 tons up the steepest grades. The first four years of their work were extremely busy, their main task being the haulage of mineral ore trains to the smelter at Zeehan. After the outbreak of the First World War the work of the locomotives became comparatively light, amounting to little more than one train per week. Nevertheless, by the 1920s, the years of hard work had taken their toll and the locomotives were in a very worn state. The TGR's Zeehan fitter therefore assembled a single locomotive from the best parts of K1 and K2.

In 1929 the Hercules mine at Williamsford, by then the tramway's principal customer, diverted its ore output to a smelter at Rosebery using a new

aerial ropeway. The wagons of ore coming down the cable-worked incline from the mine now discharged into the bunker of the aerial ropeway rather than the tramway wagons. This marked the end of the viability of the tramway which accordingly closed on 30th June 1929. Thereafter the locomotives lay out of use in their shed at Zeehan, despite several attempts by the Government Railway to sell them.

Nearly twenty years later Beyer, Peacock made enquiries to purchase the works plates of K1 and K2 for display in their proposed museum at Gorton. The request was answered with an offer of K1 itself at a scrap price. Today's railway heritage community has the enthusiasm of a young Tasmanian Railways engineer, Charles S Smith, who was later to become Chief Engineer, to thank for this intervention. Fortunately the offer was accepted by Beyer, Peacock and the locomotive was shipped to Gorton. Unfortunately the hope that it could be returned to running order was never realised by Beyer, Peacock.

Above Right: *K1 was returned to Gorton in 1948 for preservation by Beyer, Peacock. Partially restored, it stood in the workshops until their closure in the 1960s.* (Neville Fields, Manchester Locomotive Society Collection)

Above: *K1 was offered to the FR Society for £1000 on the closure of Gorton works. It was displayed for two years at Porthmadog Harbour Station.* (K1 Group Collection)

Below: *Approaching the end of its restoration, K1 moved out of Boston Lodge under its own steam on 7 September 2004.* (Peter Johnson)

Right: *With the adoption of K1 as a restoration project by the WHR Society the locomotive was moved from display at the National Railway Museum to Tyseley Locomotive Works. Project Leader Colin Hill provides a guided tour of the work in progress. The boiler cradle is in the foreground.* (K1 Group Collection)

Below: *K1 was loaned to the National Railway Museum, York, from 1976 to April 1995. It was displayed in lined grey livery, with the buffer beams and balance weights picked out in red. The locomotive is seen on 25th August 1982, standing on a standard gauge Weltrol wagon on the turntable at the centre of the roundhouse locomotive display.* (David Payling)

Left: *In March 2004 the firebox backhead was being fitted out with its many items of equipment.* (Roy Woods)

Below: *The restoration work was transferred to Boston Lodge in 2000. By 13th March 2004 K1 was nearing completion in the erecting shop. This view from the front bogie shows the smokebox with the blast pipe and blower ring in place. Also prominent on the top left of the smokebox wrapper is the change valve. This allows the driver to admit live steam to the front, low pressure bogie to assist a difficult start.* (Roy Woods)

It was reassembled and placed on display in the machine shop at the works, cosmetically restored. The engine was eventually sold to the FR Society for £1000 on the closure of the Gorton works in 1966.

From 1966 K1 enjoyed a long period of display, first at Porthmadog and then at York, as described in the Introduction. From the earliest days of the Welsh Highland Railway Society K1 has been regarded as a symbol of the railway's future. In 1995 the removal of K1 from the National Railway Museum was negotiated and, after a brief period of display in Caernarfon and at Minffordd, it was moved to the premises of the Tyseley Locomotive Works. Here a group of WHR Society volunteers had

Above: *The completed locomotive first appeared in traffic as an oil burner. In this form it was a guest of honour at the Crewe Works Open Day on 10th September 2005.* (Roy Woods)

Below: *K1 made its first trip to Rhyd Ddu on 8th September 2006. Members of the restoration team were on the train and were photographed on arrival at the temporary terminus.* (Roy Woods)

Right: *The first journey to Rhyd Ddu saw K1 bedecked with celebratory flags, seen here to advantage as the locomotive ran round its train for the return journey.* (Roy Woods)

undertaken to restore the locomotive for use on the rebuilt railway. This was a key commitment in the Society's support for the overall project to rebuild the WHR. The "K1 Group" began the task of stripping down the locomotive to its components for overhaul, replacement or repair. Items which ultimately had to be replaced included the two pivot assemblies, one between the frames of each bogie, which were heavily corroded. They were replaced by new welded fabrications riveted in place between the frame plates. The eight axleboxes too were very worn and patterns were made and cast for new boxes. The boiler was corroded, the front ring and the second ring of the barrel proving to be beyond repair. It was decided to raise funds for a new boiler which was completed in 2002 by Israel Newton of Bradford.

During the period at Tyseley another component, the compounding "change valve," was overhauled. It proved quite immovable with the equipment available, being solidly seized. The neighbouring British Railways workshop fortunately was able to make its press available and a pressure of 30 tons was eventually required to release the core of the valve. The change valve serves as a fall back measure for the

Above: *K1 hauling one of the Santa trains on 23 December 2007.* (Peter Johnson)

Right: *K1 climbing towards Nantmor on 17 May 2009.* (Peter Johnson)

Left: *Partially dismantled, K1 in Dinas carriage shed on 5 October 2019.* (Peter Johnson)

Lower Left: *K1 as restored to service on the Statfold Barn Railway on 8 August 2020, its first public appearance.* (Peter Johnson)

Bottom: *Another view of K1 at the Statfold Barn Railway, seen operating on 13 June 2021.* (Peter Johnson)

footplate crew if difficulties arise in getting a heavy train under way. Operation of the valve admits live steam to the low pressure cylinders to help get the train moving. This is achieved by operating a valve on the right hand side of the smokebox which supplies live steam to a piston and cylinder inside the front low pressure bogie. The steam pressure forces the piston to move the change valve from its compound setting to its live steam setting. When the piston has completed its movement it uncovers a port which diverts a supply of live steam to the low

Top Right: *With the cost of fuel oil rising rapidly K1 was converted to coal firing by the 2007 season. The first coal rails proved to be too short to allow enough coal to be carried for a day's work. On the morning of 9th September 2007 the locomotive stood in the Dinas running shed alongside No.143, being prepared for the railway's Superpower event.* (Steve Sedgwick)

Lower Right: *The mountains were still in the grip of wintry weather at the start of the 2008 running season. On 6th April K1 was photographed approaching Rhyd Ddu, beneath the waste tips of the Rhosclogwyn slate quarry, with the bulk of Snowdon itself in the background.* (Steve Sedgwick)

Below: *The year 2009 was the centenary of the building of the world's first Garratt locomotives, K1 and K2, at Beyer, Peacock's Gorton foundry. To mark the occasion the Manchester Museum of Science and Industry held an exhibition. K1 was the star of the day, exhibited on a low loader. Notice the lining that enhances K1's black livery.* (David Payling)

pressure cylinder valve chests. In its "compound" (normal) setting the change valve routes steam exhausted from the high pressure cylinders of the rear bogie via the condenser pipe between the bogies into the low pressure cylinder valve chests whence it is re-used in the low pressure cylinders. Exhaust steam from the low pressure cylinders is routed to the chimney. When the valve is in its "simple" position the exhaust from the high pressure cylinders is routed to the chimney whilst the low pressure valve chests and cylinders are powered by high pressure steam.

The work of restoration was transferred from Birmingham to Boston Lodge in 2000 and the locomotive gradually reassembled as finances and volunteer resources permitted. On 22nd August 2004 steam was raised in the new boiler and, for the first time since 1929, K1 moved under its own power.

Top: *On 17th August the low loader trailer made a journey to K1's birthplace at Gorton.* (Michael Chapman)

Inset: *The Institution of Mechanical Engineers marked the occasion of the locomotive's centenary with an Engineering Heritage Award.* (K1 Group)

Left: *This fine 7¼ inch gauge model of K1 built by Milner Engineering in 1987/8 was displayed in the Statfold Barn Railway's museum in 2020.* (Peter Johnson)

Above: *The Superpower weekend of 13th September 2009 saw K1 traversing the Aberglaslyn Pass with a train of Ffestiniog and Welsh Highland heritage carriages.* (Roy Woods)

Left: *With Llyn y Gader and the pass to the Nantlle valley in the background K1, with a train of ex-SAR freight vehicles, passes Pitt's Head on a photo charter on 28th February 2011.* (Ralph Ward)

During the Autumn the locomotive was moved by road to Dinas for running in and for rectification of any snags. The new axleboxes proved to be a particular source of difficulty, one in particular persistently running warm. With re-alignment of the boxes and improvements to their lubrication system the problem was overcome. Stiffness of the regulator valve was addressed by the addition of a displacement lubricator (the regulator valve on K1 is unusual in that it is located not in the dome of the locomotive but in a housing on top of the firebox in front of the spectacle plate). The live steam supply pipe from the regulator housing to the high pressure bogie runs beneath raised lagging around the left hand firebox shoulder and down into the cab before passing through the floor into the rear bogie steam chests. Another modification has been the fitting of new steam sanding arrangements in place of the sanding originally fitted. The original sanding had been supplemented in Tasmania with large sand containers fitted on the top of the water tank to give extra adhesion on this difficult and steeply graded route. For service in North Wales compressed air sanding equipment recovered from British Railways Class 08 shunters has proved ideal for achieving adhesion on a slippery rail by creating a controlled jet of steam-propelled sand under the outer wheels of each bogie.

The effective entry of the locomotive into regular WHR service was with the Santa Trains at Caernarfon leading up to Christmas 2007. These were worked entirely by K1 as were the schools' half term trains, which were run during a fortnight in February 2008. Changes in fuel economics

The finished article! On 21st February 2011, K1 departs from the coaling facilities at Porthmadog Harbour. It proudly displays its fully lined out black livery and a replica of the original headlight.
(Michael Chapman)

meant that the oil firing fitted to K1 during its restoration was switched to coal firing which, by 2007, had become much less expensive than oil. The locomotive has been found to steam very well on coal. Coal rails were added to increase the capacity of the rear bunker. Replica brass headlights were made, to the same appearance as the originals from 1909, lit electrically by a steam turbo generator. In Winter 2007, NG/G16 Garratt No.138 was taken out of service for its 10 years boiler overhaul. As a result, in 2008, K1 experienced a busy season. Under test, with improved valve settings K1 hauled an 11 car test train between Caernarfon and Waunfawr but at the reported expense of track damage caused by its short-wheelbase bogies. It was not able to to take a place alongside the NGG16s.

The new and exciting future forecast by David Payling for K1 in 2012 turned out not to be on the WHR but in Staffordshire, on the Statfold Barn Railway. In Wales it soon became clear that the modern WHR had no place for K1, the loads of both peak and off-peak services being too great for it. After a few gala appearances it was stored at Dinas, and dismantling in preparation for its 10-year boiler exam was started.

In 2019 agreement was reached for it to be displayed at the Staffordhsire line. Once there its boiler exam was undertaken and it was repainted, making its first public appearance in steam on 8 August 2020. At its new home, shared with many other historic narrow gauge locomotives, it has been a popular attraction.

Over the Welsh Highland Railway's AGM weekend in 2021 several extra trains were run for society members as a 'thank you' for the support given to the railway during the pandemic. A significant attraction was the operation of K1, visiting from the Statfold Barn Railway. It was photographed at Caernarfon following a run to Rhyd Ddu on 17 September.
(Peter Johnson)

- VIII -
History of the WHR NG/G16 Beyer Garratts

~ *Introduction* ~

The motive power requirement for a revived Welsh Highland Railway has been described in the Introduction to this book. Taking the example of the pattern of Ffestiniog Railway services, the present day requirement at Porthmadog is for a six-car coaching set as the standard train. On busy days the requirement for passenger accommodation for the jurney to Blaenau Ffestiniog can frequently raise this to a total train length of ten to twelve cars. The gradients of the Ffestiniog are at an average of approximately 1 in 80. In contrast, the Welsh Highland Railway gradients are twice as steep as this and stretch over many miles. These include the climb out of Caernarfon to Dinas at gradients touching on 1 in 60 and on from Dinas to Tryfan Junction at 1 in 40 faced by Porthmadog-bound trains. For Caernarfon-bound trains, there is the long climb at 1 in 40 from Hafod-y-Llyn to Pont Cae'r Gors. On the FR a double Fairlie is permitted a train of up to twelve cars on the 1 in 80. Clearly a train of similar length on the doubly steep gradients of the WHR would require a more powerful motive power source.

In the early 1990s the search for affordable motive power to meet the needs of the re-born WHR was far ranging and led eventually to South Africa. Here, the authorities were no longer supporting the steam-powered narrow gauge. Four, out of a total of five narrow gauge lines, amounting to more than 200 miles of railway, had been closed and demolished since the early 1980s. One such closed line, from Port Shepstone to Harding, had been re-opened in 1988 as a freight and tourist passenger business. This was the newly constituted Alfred County Railway. The company had acquired access to much of the rolling stock assets of the four closed SAR lines in Natal. In the early 1990s the ACR had entered an agreement with Spoornet, the successor to South African Railways. This included the replacement of the ACR's frequently double-headed NG/G16 power for its timber traffic with the use of hired-in Class 91 diesel electric power. This had made many Beyer-Garratt locomotives surplus to requirements.

The Ffestiniog management discovered that some of the surplus engines were available for sale. A contract was placed for the purchase and overhaul of two locomotives. They were Nos.138 and 143, the latter being chosen for its historical significance rather than for its condition which was quite run down. In fact, a total of five engines were tentatively reserved for the Project. They included Nos.139 and 142 from the 1958 batch and either No.149 or 151 from the mechanically very similar 1968 Hunslet Taylor batch.

This early plan was overtaken by events, including the unexpected donation to the WHR of sister locomotive No.140 by its consortium of European owners. While 140 has yet to see service in its own right, its power bogies and other components have been used on other locos, one of the benefits of operating a standard fleet. Later, Nos 87 and 130 were acquired by sponsors and restored for use on the WHR as described later.

~ No.87 (Cockerill, 3267, 1936) ~

No.87 is the oldest of the NG/G16s in service on the WHR. It was built by John Cockerill of Seraing, Belgium, in 1936 as Works No. 3267, Boiler Number 8786. Of the four engines built in 1936 the other three are currently at Sandstone in South Africa. No.88 has been restored to steam and runs at Sandstone in the green livery it once carried for the Banana Express tourist train at Port Shepstone. In appearance the 1936 Cockerill locomotives closely resemble the twelve NG/G13s built in 1927-8 by Hanomag of Germany. Indeed, as newly delivered in 1937, they were regarded as NG/G13s! The four Cockerill NG/G16s had cabs of the same size as the NG/G13s with no window to the rear of the side doorway.

Left: *This early right hand cab-side view of No.87 shows the original number plate to have been replaced by one identifying the locomotive as a NG/G16. The foot rest for the driver's swing-out seat shares the bolt hole of the number plate. The cab side and hand rail had no bulge to give clearance for the driver's hand when using the reversing handle. The heat of the cramped cab interior is added to by the vacuum brake exhauster and the two sight feed lubricators which are visible through the open cab window.*
(Neil Mardell, NGRS Archive)

Below: *On 5th May 1971 No.87 was at rest at Ixopo running shed on the Donnybrook line. By this time the original sanding arrangements on this 35 years old engine had been replaced by sand boxes mounted on the ends of the tank and bunker. It still carried its original, lipped Beyer, Peacock chimney but the whistle mounting had switched to the steam manifold next to the cab spectacle plate.*
(Leith Paxton)

Left: *On 21st March 1986, fewer than four months before final closure of the Donnybrook line, No.87 heads a freight from Ixopo to Donnybrook through Maxwell station.* (Dick Manton)

Below: *On 2nd September 1972 No.87 suffered a derailment near to Highflats on the Umzinto branch in Natal. The accident occurred on a sharp left hand curve, leaving the locomotive lying on its right hand side in the ballast. This view was of great use during the recent restoration of the engine at Boston Lodge, showing the lay-out of the pipe work beneath the engine which was normally hidden from sight.* (Terry Hutson, SA Rail collection)

Right: *After the September 1972 accident No.87 was eventually jacked upright, the jacks being applied to the base of the dome.* (Terry Hutson, SA Rail collection)

No.87 was delivered new, together with sister engine No.88, to Port Shepstone in April 1937. Detailed allocation history has not so far come to light but it is believed that No.87 worked largely at Port Shepstone until 1968. After this, there is photographic evidence to show that it worked on most of the Natal branches before its withdrawal in 1986. In March 1972 it was photographed at work on the mid-Illovo branch. Later that year, however, it was in service on the Donnybrook line where, on the 2nd September, it was the victim of a derailment on a sharp left hand curve, coming to rest on its right hand side at the top of an embankment. This mishap is said to have been fatal for at least one of the crew. Despite extensive recent enquiries the detailed circumstances remain unknown. The locomotive was jacked upright, re-railed and returned to service after receiving repairs to its right hand side platework. This included patches to the bunker side and a whole new cab side, the latter including a bulge to accommodate the reversing handle, normally seen only on post war NG/G16s.

Above: *Highflats was a servicing and hand-over point for trains some six hours from Umzinto on the way to Ixopo and Donnybrook. No.87 has arrived with a train from Ixopo on 21st January 1981. The fire is being cleaned and water tanks replenished before its return to Ixopo with freight from Umzinto.* (Tony Leeson)

Above Left: *No.87 passes Mabedlana on the Donnybrook line with a short freight train of agricultural produce on 26th January 1986.* (Tony Leeson)

Left: *Two locomotives eventually destined to find their way to North Wales stand rusting and abandoned at Donnybrook on 8th October 1986. In the foreground No.109 remains relatively complete except for its cab-side number plates, whilst No.87 stands at the water column in the background.* (Tony Leeson)

No. 87 at Boston Lodge on 24 February 2006, ready for its restoration to start. (Peter Johnson)

After its final Durban workshop repair in August 1977 No.87 returned to the Donnybrook line. It now carried the oldest existing boiler, the NG/G13 boiler fitted originally to the class pioneer, No.58, in 1927, which it still carries today. At Donnybrook it was one of the last two locomotives to remain serviceable and was slated to haul the last train on the line in July 1986. This honour, however, went to No.113 owing to a hot box which had developed on No.87. Thereafter the locomotive stood out of use and was systematically robbed of valuable metal castings and pipework. In January 1998 it was eventually bought for the abortive Robin Hood's Bay Railway scheme in Yorkshire. When this scheme was cancelled, it was sold to the Exmoor Steam Railway in December 1998.

In late 2005 No.87 stands forlornly at the Exmoor Steam Centre. On examination by F&WHR representatives it was judged to be the better prospect for restoration of the two available Garratt locomotives. (David Payling collection)

Top Left: *Once inside Boston Lodge depth testing showed that the firebox backhead had wasted from its original 15mm thickness to 3mm in places since its birth in Hanomag's workshops in 1927! The solution was to cut off the outer and inner firebox backs and to weld in new platework. The new outer firebox back can be seen leaning on the right of the firebox.* (David Payling)

Top Centre: *On 31st March 2008 the firebox was complete, the new stay heads being visible on the backplate. The wash-out plugs are visible at the top and bottom of the side plates.* (David Payling)

Top Right: *The wooden pattern for the Beyer, Peacock chimney, donated by an ex-employee, had been used to cast a chimney to the original pattern.* (David Payling)

Left: *At the front of the workshop the trailing bogie was nearing completion, the cylinder cladding remaining to be fitted. The white painted fly cranks, with their cast-in balance weights, are prominent.* (David Payling)

Right: *In October 2008 the white painted tank and bunker were ready for fitting, the former being the original whilst the latter had been fabricated by Brunswick Ironworks, Caernarfon, to replace the corroded original.* (Roy Woods)

Centre Right: *The pattern for casting the brass cab-side plates was made by a WHRS member. A combination of measuring the distance between the actual screw holes on the cab side sheet and studying a close-up photograph of the locomotive when in South Africa produced the dimensions. It seemed appropriate to use the later NG/G16 design rather than the 1936 NG/G13 version, although the original Dutch language version has been retained.* (David Payling)

Centre Far Right: *The ends of the bunker and water tank carry small brass plates showing the engine's running number.* (David Payling)

Bottom Right: *The bronze data plate on No.87's smoke box reveals that this engine currently carries the boiler (No.7850) of the pioneer NG/G13 locomotive, No.58, built by Hanomag in 1927! The bottom row of data show the dates of its annual SAR hydraulic tests, the last being June 1986. The edge of the plate shows the stamped two month's extension to August. This allowed it to share in hauling the final trains on the Umzinto branch in Natal to be worked before closure.* (David Payling)

Above: *On 31st January 2009, under a stormy sky, the completed locomotive was photographed at its first appearance outside the workshops in Boston Lodge yard.* (Roger Dimmick)

Left: *By 9th April No.87 was in service, seen here at Dinas, heading a quiet, early season train for Beddgelert.* (David Payling)

Below: *The locomotive was transferred from Boston Lodge to Dinas on 23rd March, pausing for photographs at the Network Rail crossing in Porthmadog. Network Rail officials and F&WHR staff were in attendance. General Manager Paul Lewin is on the footplate whilst the long-standing Permanent Way manager, Fred Howes, is on the far right.* (Andrew Thomas)

The purchase and workshop restoration of No.87 for service on the Welsh Highland Railway has been funded by a sponsor who became interested in the locomotives being offered for sale by the ESR in 2004. Restoration was started at Boston Lodge in 2006. On 23 March 2009 No. 87 became the first steam locomotive to transfer from the FR to the WHR on its own wheels. Entering service later in 2009, expenditure had exceeded half a million pounds.

Returned to a close approximation of its original appearance, any changes being determined by operational factors for its work in passenger service.

During the restoration at Boston Lodge many new patterns were required to allow the casting of replacement fittings for those removed before the locomotive reached the UK. One such is the handsome Beyer, Peacock chimney. The pattern for this had been donated by a member of staff of the company who had rescued it on the closure of Gorton works in 1966. This has allowed the casting of a new chimney of authentic design, rather than a plain SAR flower pot shaped chimney as carried by the other NG/G16s in North Wales. Another item to require extensive repairs has been the boiler, some parts of which are now over 80 years old.

Above: *There are few stations in the world where Beyer-Garratts pass each other on passenger trains. In 2009, 21st August was a glorious summer's day. No.87 waits with its train at Waunfawr for No.143 to clear the block section to Rhyd Ddu with its Caernarfon-bound train.* (David Payling)

Right: *The new Halt at Meillionen was nearing completion on 8th April as No.87 passes with a Beddgelert-bound train.* (David Payling)

Above: *No.87 rests at Beddgelert on a sunny 8th April 2009. This station is unusual in that it was not possible for the original engineers in the 1900s to achieve a horizontal layout, the prevailing gradient of 1 in 40 continuing through the platforms. Because of this the guard will have applied the train hand brake before signalling to the driver that the locomotive can be uncoupled to run round for the return to Caernarfon.* (David Payling)

The whole of the firebox inner and outer backhead had to be replaced by new platework when depth gauging showed the originally 15-16mm thick outer back head to have become as thin as 3mm in places. A whole new bunker and cab have been constructed. A full set of the original SAR-Cockerill drawings was obtained from South Africa to help with the restoration, the purchase being one of the last transactions of the Transnet Heritage Library in Johannesburg before its permanent closure.

Rather than reconstruct the sight feed lubrication equipment, No.87 has been fitted out with mechanical lubricators on the buffer beams of each bogie, as on Nos.138 and 143. The bogies have also been enhanced by the fitting of cab-operated steam sanding adapted from components recovered from scrapped BR Class 08 diesel shunters. The firebox has also been equipped with a rocking grate and an updated spark-proofed ash pan. Together, these modifications have allowed the locomotive to be coal fired in service.

The locomotive emerged from Boston Lodge in January 2009. After initial trials it entered service in time for the 2009 running season. The livery carried for its first year in service was similar to the grey primer of works photos although the paint was normal locomotive paint. There were a number of teething problems including the valve settings. With these corrected the locomotive is proving to be a very capable performer on the Welsh Highland. For 2010 the locomotive was finished in its long term livery of deep blue, similar to that carried some years ago by the Ffestiniog's Hunslet *Linda*.

Following a ten-year boiler exam and mechanical overhaul completed in 2020 No. 87 was turned out in a black livery that acknowledged its service in South Africa.

Right: *With the tank front adorned with a red "L" plate, an early test train sees No.87 approaching the level crossing at Nantmor. It has just left the long tunnel out of the Aberglaslyn Pass and crossed the high embankment through Cwm Bychan.* (Roy Woods)

Below: *Snowdon forms the background as No.87 with its nine-car train passes the waste tips of Rhosclogwyn slate quarry on the approach to Rhyd Ddu.* (David Payling)

Above: *For the 2010 running season the engine was repainted into a deep blue livery lined in white against a black background. On 28th May it was captured on camera at Pont Croesor with a Caernarfon-bound train, double heading with No.138.* (F&WHR Co.)

Right: *On 10th October 2010 No.87 has just arrived at Porthmadog Harbour Station with a train from the WHR. The locomotive makes a contrast in size with newly completed L&BR replica 2-6-2T 'Lyd', acting as station pilot for Caernarfon trains.* (Peter Treloar)

No.87 in blue livery, waits for 'Lyd' to clear the section at Beddgelert on a very rainy day in September 2010. The weather makes a direct contrast with the prevailing conditions in South Africa! (Peter Treloar)

Right: *When HM the Queen and HRH the Duke of Edinburgh visited the WHR on 27 April 2010 No. 87 was selected to haul the royal train. It is seen awaiting the arrival of the royal party at Caernarfon.* (Peter Johnson)

Below: *Looking as though they belong. No. 143 and No. 87, separated by the water bowser, approach Rhyd Ddu in September 2018.* (Chris Parry)

Left: *No. 87 in its new black livery heading for Beddgelert on 18 August 2020, one of the small number of trains that ran during the year.* (Chris Parry)

~ No.109 (Beyer, Peacock 6919, 1939) ~

In 1939, Beyer, Peacock received an order from SAR for eight NG/G16s. Although almost identical with the four John Cockerill Garratts of 1936, the design was now enhanced with a cab extended some five inches rearwards, recognisable by the addition of a hinged window to the rear of the cab doorway. On completion, the first three engines of the batch, Nos.109-111, were shipped to Port Elizabeth, arriving in April for work on the Avontuur Branch. The remaining five, Nos.112-116, were shared between the Natal branches at Umzinto and Port Shepstone. At Port Elizabeth No.109's main work was powering the very heavy limestone trains whose journey began with the tough climb of the twelve miles of the 1 in 40 bank from Loerie to Summit, on the way to Chelsea Junction near Port Elizabeth. It also hauled mixed trains of general merchandise as well as fruit to the docks for export. General overhauls saw transfer of the locomotive, loaded piggyback on a pair of Cape gauge bogie wagons, to the workshops at Uitenhage. During one at least of these overhauls the boiler from a post-war engine was fitted. This can be seen in some of the photographs, the clack boxes being mounted on the front ring of the boiler, rather than just ahead of the dome. Also the steam manifold is further forward, away from the cab, with the safety valves side by side in front of it.

In 1961 the whole class of 21 NG15 locomotives arrived at Port Elizabeth from the Otavi Branch in Namibia. This had the result of allowing seven of the resident Garratts to be transferred away to Natal. However, No.109 was one of those to remain, mainly for the limestone traffic, receiving various modifications in the years that followed. One of the more noticeable was the removal of the sand box mounted on the water tank top. This arrangement was vulnerable to wetting of the sand during replenishment of the water tank and was now replaced by sand boxes mounted in pairs on the ends of the bunker and water tank. Other changes included the replacement of the handsome Beyer, Peacock chimney with a SAR flower pot variety. The Stone Tonum headlight was replaced by twin sealed beam lights. The riveted tank and bunker were renewed with all-welded fabrications.

In 1973, when the fleet of 20 newly built General Electric Class 91 diesel electrics arrived at Port Elizabeth, most of the remaining Garratts were

Right: *No.109 stands at Humewood Road depot on 5th March 1966. It still carried the handsome Stone Tonum headlight, Beyer, Peacock chimney, its original riveted tank and bunker, plus the sand box mounted on the tank top. The boiler had been replaced during workshop repair with a post-war example, although the vacuum brake ejector and lubricators remained inside the cab as built.* (Leith Paxton)

Inset: *The cab-side number plate shows no NG prefix; all the NG/G13s and the pre-war NG/G16s being numbered in this way.* (Neil Mardell, NGRS Archive)

transferred to Natal. No.109 was allocated to the Umzinto to Donnybrook line, located approximately midway between Port Shepstone and Durban. This 97½ mile branch had no mineral traffic. The main freight was timber from the vast plantations in the hills around Ixopo and Donnybrook, plus farm produce and also sugar cane from the coastal plain near Umzinto. Overhauls were carried out at the Pietermaritzburg workshops near Durban. At its final SAR overhaul in April 1976 No.109 received the NG/G13 boiler (Hanomag 8387, 1928) which it carries today. It was eventually taken out of service in July 1985 on expiry of its boiler certificate, by which time workshop overhauls of steam engines had ceased. Meanwhile a severe tropical storm (named Demoina) had struck the Natal coast on 29th January 1984, causing eight serious washouts on the coastal section of the line between Umzinto and Highflats. Although repaired, the line between Ixopo and Umzinto was nearing its closure to traffic, soon becoming truncated at Highflats. The rest of the Donnybrook system was progressively closed down over the following two years, a final excursion from Ixopo to Donnybrook being hauled on 12th July 1986 by sister locomotive No.113. After that No.109 lay derelict with sisters Nos. 87, 113, and 153 at Donnybrook. In the early 1990s the four were donated to the Midmar Historic Village near Pietermaritzburg where a narrow gauge railway had been planned. In the event, No.109 did not go to Midmar, being instead placed in storage at Springs, near Johannesburg. It was later inspected and purchased by the Stirland family for the Exmoor Steam Railway. It arrived at Tilbury Docks in June 1995, becoming the first NG/G16 to come to Britain for preservation.

Above: *On 13th January 1973 No.109 was specially cleaned for Apple Express duty. It is seen here on the return jouney, climbing Loerie bank, still fitted with its Beyer, Peacock chimney but now carrying a post-war boiler and a new welded front water tank. The American Pyle headlight from Leith Paxton's collection completes the picture.* (Leith Paxton)

Above: *On its new home line, from Umzinto to Donnybrook, No.109 hurries a train of a guard's van and ten B wagons loaded with pulp wood towards Kenterton. This type of wagon was awkward and tedious to load with timber and hence very unpopular with farmers.* (Neville Fields)

Below: *In this 1973 photograph No.109 is seen loaded onto Cape Gauge flat cars. It has been partly dismantled for the journey from Port Elizabeth to Natal to give clearance beneath the overhead line equipment on the way. In the background an NG15 edges down the viaduct from the narrow gauge station and depot above with a train of fruit for the docks whilst a Cape Gauge Class S2 shunter takes water.* (Leith Paxton)

Above: *No.109 stands outside Ixopo shed on 5th September 1980. The engine was by this time almost the same in its detail fittings as those from post war batches, the exception being the continued use of sight feed lubrication rather than mechanical lubricators on the buffer beams.* (Neville Fields)

Right: *The Stirland family bought No.109 for the Exmoor Steam Railway in 1986. During the purchase the fitters at Springs, near Johannesburg, had mistakenly reassembled the engine with a cab roof belonging to a NG/G13, hence the lack of fit to the rear of the cab doorway.* (Julie Stirland)

In 2009 it was announced that No.109 had been purchased by the Waterman Railway Heritage Trust. It is pictured here outside the LNWR workshop at Crewe awaiting restoration. (Waterman Railway Heritage Trust)

Above: *One of No. 109's power units on display at the National Exhibition Centre during the 2010 Warley Model Railway Exhibition.* (Peter Johnson)

In the Spring of 2009 Pete Waterman, pop record producer, railway enthusiast and then owner of Crewe-based LNWR Heritage workshops, made a visit to the FR and WHR, including the experience of a gravity slate train ride on the former, plus a spell of firing on No.87 on the WHR. Impressed by the two railways, he made arrangements for his works manager, Steve Latham, to visit Exmoor Steam, together with the FR's own Paul Lewin and Jon Whalley. They inspected the two ex-SAR locomotives on offer for sale, NG/G16 Garratts Nos.109 and 130. It was decided that No.109 would be purchased and restored by the Waterman Railway Heritage Trust at Crewe. The work would be carried out in close co-operation with Boston Lodge where much expertise had been developed through the earlier restoration of No.87. Crucially the FR owns a wealth of patterns for casting the many components lost during its ten years of storage in South Africa. One of the many items required was a new cab. In assembling the components for No.109 in 1995 at Springs depot, the fitters had mistakenly selected a cab roof from a NG/G13 (a slightly smaller cab with no window to the rear of the doorway)! With support from national and local government agencies, a training scheme was devised for twenty previously unemployed people to restore No. 109, work starting on 16 October 2009.

However, the change of government in 2010 saw funding removed and the scheme was ended prematurely. After a period of storage at Dinas, No. 109 was moved to Derbyshire and remains unrestored.

~ No.138 (Beyer, Peacock 7863, 1958) ~

Above: *The SAR service life of No.138 began at Port Shepstone in December 1958. At that time it carried the running number "E138." Correct cab-side plates were fitted later to identify the engine as NG138. It was based on the Harding branch in Natal throughout its SAR and ACR working life. It is seen here in close-up at Port Shepstone depot in the early 1960s.* (A Spit, NGRS archive)

Right: *The Beyer, Peacock works plate of No.138.* (Tony Leeson)

Garratt No.138 is the second of the seven engines built by Beyer, Peacock to the order of the Tsumeb Mining Corporation of South West Africa (Namibia) in 1958. When imminent gauge broadening of the line to Tsumeb made the locomotives superfluous, this triggered the SAR's agreement to purchase them from the Corporation for use elsewhere on the South African narrow gauge. Before entering SAR service the Tsumeb cab-side plates (TC7) were replaced by SAR plates. No.138 thus entered traffic at Port Shepstone with cab-side number plates reading "E138." The reason why Nos.137 - 140 initially carried cab-side plates with an "E" prefix was that in 1958 the brass foundry at the Pietermaritzburg workshops was producing plates mainly for newly built Cape gauge electric locomotives. The foundry had incorrectly assumed that Nos.137 to 140 were also electrics! The engine became a long standing resident of the 76 miles long Port Shepstone to Harding line, receiving most of its routine maintenance and intermediate repairs at Port Shepstone depot.

The maintenance records of No.138 have survived and are now part of the archive of information at Boston Lodge. They had arrived in Wales along with the locomotive after its purchase for the WHR and refurbishment by the Alfred County Railway in 1997. The records include the complete set of SAR Boiler Certificates stretching back to its delivery as a new locomotive by rail to Port Shepstone on 3rd December 1958. Another record to survive is the Master Boiler Logbook of boiler inspections

Left: *A rear view of E138 shows the contrast in its size with Cape gauge GCA Garratt No. 2614 on the adjacent siding.* (A Spit, NGRS archive)

Below: *Surrounded by Zulu homes with their conical roofs No.138 heads a Harding-bound freight through Bomela in March 1986. The load consists of sheeted agricultural supplies plus the rare inclusion of some wagons of cattle.* (Dick Manton)

and repairs, stretching from the last general repair on 27th July 1981 to the end of SAR ownership on 4th July 1986.

The engine had been delivered carrying Beyer, Peacock boiler No.7036, which was certified by SAR on 28th November 1958 at Durban. It was carried by the locomotive until its first major workshop overhaul ten years later at Pietermaritzburg. After each of its three SAR general workshop repairs the locomotive was returned to traffic with a different boiler, as detailed in the accompanying table. After the first repair it re-entered traffic at Port Shepstone on 21st November 1968. The second general repair was undertaken in 1973, the locomotive being released to traffic at Port Shepstone on 14th November. Its third and final SAR general repair took place in 1981 and it re-entered traffic on 27th July carrying boiler No.7114. This was a Hunslet boiler constructed in Leeds in 1968 as a spare boiler for the batch of eight Hunslet Taylor NG/G16s constructed that year. In 1981 boiler No.7114 had been repaired with a new welded steel firebox. It was common for the Natal Garratts to be switched between the four narrow gauge branches in the State. However, the boiler certificates show that No.138 was based at Port Shepstone throughout its South African working life.

Above Right: *Izingolweni was an important servicing point for steam trains in SAR and ACR days. Here No.138 has its fire cleaned on 15th August 1986. The cab-side plates of a number of locomotives based at Port Shepstone were customised, with a green central background.* (Tony Leeson)

Below: *Several Garratts can be seen on shed in this March 1986 scene. No.138 stands on the right, still carrying small "E138" plates on the tank and bunker ends.* (Dick Manton)

BOILER CHRONOLOGY for No.138

Workshop Repair	Date	Boiler Number	Date First Used	First Fitted to:
(New)	December 1958	7036	1958	No.138
General	November 1968	7039	1958	No.141
General	November1973	7019	1950	No.131
General	July 1981	7114	(1968)	Spare Boiler

Boiler No.7114 was carried by No.138 for its first ten years on the WHR. After withdrawal for a boiler overhaul in 2007, it returned to traffic in 2009 with the same boiler.

The Locomotive Repair Book, used by footplate crews to log faults, has also reached Boston Lodge. Each pair of pages records footplate crew complaints on the left whilst the right hand page was reserved for the fitter's response to each problem. Alfred County Railway operations commenced on 3rd December 1987 and this record stretches through the ACR period from 3rd January 1988 to the engine being taken out of traffic on 15th January 1991. The Repair Book records all the small problems of steam engines in daily use, scarcely a day going by without some comment. A constant task for the fitters was to re-pack leaking piston and piston valve spindle glands. Leaking cylinder cocks were another frequent cause of complaint, not to mention leaking valve spindles among the many controls on the footplate. Another complaint was the need for brake adjustment or brake block renewal. Locomotives on the timber trains from Harding to Port Shepstone would require new

Right: *On 21st December 1990 the ACR's Port Shepstone shunter was No.138, carrying a Beyer, Peacock works plate and small number plates on its front and back, both prefixed with "E." The cab-side plates had disappeared after the closure of the line by SATS.* (Tony Leeson)

Above: *No.138 nears the end of its overhaul at the Port Shepstone depot of the Alfred County Railway in Autumn 1995.* (Jon Whalley)

Above right: *The Port Shepstone depot fitters enjoy an early test run with No.138 along the line towards Beach Halt. Phil Girdlestone inspects the motion of the hind bogie.* (Jon Whalley)

Right: *The ACR's veteran driver George van Niekerk is at the controls of No.138 on a test run early in 1996. It was later decided to reconstruct the rather battered original cabs with new platework on both Nos.138 and 143.* (Jon Whalley)

Left: *On 19th March 1996 the Ffestiniog Travel Special returned from Harding to Port Shepstone. It is seen here on its way towards Izingolweni with Nos. 138 and 155 in charge, each accompanied by a water tank car and followed by a B wagon of coal.* (Tony Leeson)

cast iron brake blocks after just four round trips, despite the trains being continuously braked! The boiler water gauges also generated their share of problems with leaking or blocked valves and pipes.

During Alfred County Railway days No.138 was initially employed as the depot shunter at Port Shepstone. This use continued for approximately two years until the three Bagnall 0-6-0 DM shunters arrived from Rustenburg platinum mines to take over shunting work. No.138 was then taken out of service and stored at Paddock in January 1991 owing to its worn tyres. At the minimum tyre thickness (29mm) the rotational speed of the wheels of a NG/G16 prevented satisfactory wheel balance and caused the locomotive to ride very roughly. The one venture of No.138 up the line beyond Port Shepstone during this period therefore was the result of a locomotive availability crisis.

After selection for the WHR project No.138 was removed from storage at Paddock in October 1994 and entered the depot workshops at Port Shepstone for its overhaul. The appearance of the original cab reflected its service of more than thirty years. It was therefore decided to replace the rather battered steel platework with new fabrication. By New Year 1996 the locomotive was nearing completion and a first oil fired steam test was carried out on 28th February. In SAR black livery, but lettered WHR on the bunker sides, it successfully hauled Ffestiniog Travel's train from Port Shepstone to Harding with over forty enthusiasts aboard on 18th March 1996. The train was double headed with No.155, one of Phil Girdlestone's two NG/G16A producer gas conversions.

Left: *The special train organised by Ffestiniog Travel is seen here on 18th March 1996 with No.138 and Phil Girdlestone's NG/G16A, No.155, in charge. The train is just at the end of Wilson's cutting.* (Tony Leeson)

On a rainy 25th October 1996 freshly overhauled No.138 was in charge of the Port Shepstone yard shunt. It was awaiting shipment from Durban to its new home in North Wales.
(Peter Bagshawe)

Left: *Hunslet 2-4-0STT* Linda *prepares to transfer one of No. 138's power units from Minffordd to Boston Lodge on 15 January 1997.* (Peter Johnson)

Below Left: *The first major Garratt components to reach Boston Lodge, No. 138's power units, seen on 16 January 1997.* (Peter Johnson)

Above Right: *Volunteers work on No. 138's boiler and cradle at Glan y Pwll On 30 March 1997.* (Peter Johnson)

Left: *Having received attention at Boston Lodge, No. 138's power units were transferred to Glan y Pwll on 6 April 1997.* (Peter Johnson)

Left: *A Gala weekend was held at Glan-y-Pwll on the Ffestiniog Railway during the Spring Bank Holiday of May 1997. By this time No.138 was complete and in steam and able to offer a "Drive a Garratt" experience, No.140 serving as a ballast weight.* (Howard Wilson)

Below: *No.138 is named 'Millennium' on 1st March 2002. From left: Roland Doyle, General Manager, WHLR Ltd., Mick Lorkins, Millennium Commission, Roger Dick, of Mott McDonald and Michael Whitehouse, Chairman, WHLR Ltd.* (F & WHR Co.)

After acceptance tests during the Autumn it was shipped from Durban to the United Kingdom, arriving in North Wales with No.143 in January 1997. The power bogies, bunker and tank were unloaded at Minffordd yard and towed to Boston Lodge. The boilers and cradles went to Glan-y-Pwll for initial examination. Boiler inspection revealed that leaking rivets around the base of the dome required attention and this work, together with other minor boiler repairs was contracted to the Severn Valley Railway's boiler workshop team. Meanwhile, the bogies were the subject of additional work at Boston Lodge to make the locomotive ready for service.

No.138 became the first Garratt to enter service on the WHR. In its newly applied green livery it also hauled the first steam operated passenger train on the line, the 11.00 service from Caernarfon to Dinas on 12th October, 1997. The FR green livery was not to last long however, a re-paint into the lighter green of the house colours of Edison Mission Energy having been sponsored by that company. This took place in the carriage shed at Dinas over the winter of 2001, the green livery being lined in yellow against black background. Unfortunately the shade of green, produced from a sample supplied by the sponsor, was significantly different from the sponsor's house colours and the whole process had to be repeated to achieve the correct colour. At a ceremony on St David's Day, 1st March 2002, the locomotive was named *Mileniwm* by the Mayor of Caernarfon and his wife. In attendance were Ken Allen (FR General Manager), Roland Doyle (WHRL Ltd General Manager), Michael Whitehouse (WHRL Ltd Chairman), Roger Dick (Mott McDonald), Mr David Frankland (Edison Mission Energy), and Mick Lorkins of the Millennium Commission to commemorate its major financial support of the reconstruction of the WHR (Caernarfon to Rhyd Ddu). The name plate also recorded the sponsorship of its paintwork by Edison Mission Energy. The plate on the engine's left hand side was in English language *Millennium*. The name never found much affection on the railway and the plates are no longer carried.

No.138 pauses at Waunfawr with a train for Caernarfon on 19th July 2005. The circular hole in the buffer beam to the left of the central slot was originally provided for the water pipe connection to an auxiliary tank car on the metal and ore trains from Tsumeb in the dry land of South West Africa. (David Payling)

Dinas station enjoys early Spring sunshine on 26th April 2007 as No.138 and its train await the return of the fireman with the token for the block section from Dinas to Waunfawr. (David Payling)

Above: *No.138, resplendent in its new livery, runs round the train at Pont Croesor on 28th May 2010. The new sanding arrangements can be seen below the sand boxes. The prominent ridge along the top edge of the tank was an addition to engines of this batch to prevent water splashing over onto the sand boxes at water stops.* (F&WHR)

Right: *No.138 was taken out of service for its 10-years overhaul at the end of 2007. A new tank was required to replace the corroded original and old and new stand together on an ex-SAR DZ wagon at Dinas on 9th April 2009. The new tank, fabricated by Brunswick Ironworks of Caernarfon, was awaiting the re-assembly of the locomotive.* (David Payling)

Ten years later, in 2007, the boiler certificate was running out although the locomotive had been the mainstay of services during the running season. The power bogies were also in need of attention, the rear unit especially so. The front bogie had been extensively rebuilt a few years before. Work on stripping the boiler for examination began in the last days of 2007. By the Autumn of 2008 it was clear that the boiler shell and firebox had withstood the ten years of service well and that little repair work would be necessary other than re-tubing. The WHR's water treatment was probably a significant factor in this success. A curiosity was the need to make an unusual repair to the base flange of the dome, a similar repair having been required on double Fairlie *Merddin Emrys*. Both boilers had been built by Hunslet in Leeds in 1967-8! Whilst the rear bunker was fit for further use the platework of the front tank was corroded and leaking and the tank was therefore renewed.

With the boiler certificate of No.143 due to expire a year after that of No.138, it was urgent to return No.138 to traffic. This unfortunately gave insufficient time to refurbish the bogies and the locomotive

Top: *In its new livery, close to that carried by some of the LMS Princess Coronation pacifics in the late 1930s, No.138 is on test, double heading a train with No.143 past Ynysfor towards Pont Croesor on a sunny 28th May 2010.* (F&WHR)

Above: *By 3rd June 2010 the engine was in regular service and is seen here with a Pont Croesor-bound train rounding the curve into Rhyd Ddu. The valley sides in the background stretch westwards towards Waunfawr, dominated by the waste tips of Glanrafon slate quarry.* (Roger Dimmick)

Right: *Although the 4th June 2010 was a hot Summer's day to enjoy the cool waters of the Glaslyn, No.138 appears to be the centre of attention. The train rounds the curve from Bryn-y-Felin bridge on its way through the Aberglaslyn Pass.* (Roger Dimmick)

re-entered service in the Summer of 2010. It was turned out by the workshops in a new red livery, lined yellow against a black background. The shade of red is similar to that carried in LMS days by some of the Princess Coronation pacifics. The oil firing, installed during the overhaul by the ACR in 1996, was retained. It now benefitted also from the fitting of automatic steam sanding equipment. This has proved very important on the heavy gradients between Beddgelert and Rhyd Ddu, reducing slipping and minimising the amount of the expensive special grit used. Fresh from its overhaul, No.138 had the honour of hauling the first passenger train from Caernarfon to Porthmadog and return. This took place among great celebrations on 30th October 2010, the passengers being the 'Gold and Silver' sponsors of the railway's revival. For the 2012 season the locomotive was converted to coal firing. Undergoing an extensive overhaul as the revised edition is prepared for publication, No. 138 is expected to be returned to service with boiler 7017, previously used in No. 143. A new bunker was fabricated at the Brunswick Ironworks in 2021.

Above: *After a short Winter break, No.138 was back in service early in 2011. It is seen here returning from the WHR over the Porthmadog Harbour bridge on 25th March.* (Andrew Thomas)

Left: *Two types of articulated locomotive, Mallet and Beyer-Garratt, pass at Beddgelert on 17th April 2011. The fireman of the visiting Statfold Barn Railway's Jatibarang No.9 (Jung No.4878, 1930) exchanges the token for the block section from Beddgelert to Rhyd Ddu with No.138's fireman.* (Dave Waldren)

Above: *Hauling a Santa train near Rhyd Ddu on 10 December 2017, No 138 was captured during a snow shower.* (Chris Parry)

Left: *No. 138 seen at Dinas undergoing a major overhaul in September 2021. A contractor repaired its boiler and its new smokebox used stainless steel plate to prolong its working life.* (Peter Johnson)

Below: *The late afternoon sun picks out the detail on No. 138 as it crosses the Britannia Bridge on 25 March 2011.* (Chris Parry)

~ No. 130 (Beyer, Peacock 7431, 1950) ~

The fourth NG/G16 to enter service on the Welsh Highland Railway was No. 130, a member of the 1950 batch. Like No. 87, it was imported to the UK by Simon Boak for his abortive Robin Hood's Bay scheme and sold to the Exmoor Steam Railway.

Like No. 87, No. 130's acquisition and restoration for the WHR was due to the generosity of a sponsor, in this case businessman Peter Best. A child in the 1950s, he attributes his interest in steam railways to being taken to watch trains at Carstairs Junction. Although qualified as a geologist he found success in developing, and selling, two businesses that manufactured and distributed engineering components used in the food industry.

His first ventures into steam ownership and operation came with the acquisition of a steam roller in 1984. His first steam locomotives were standard gauge machines acquired in 1992, both of which he restored to working order. Since then, he has

Above: *By November 2018 recognisable components, including the cab, were starting to appear at Dinas.*
(Peter Best Collection)

Below: *No. 130's new boiler after delivery at Dinas, June 2019.*
(Peter Best Collection)

restored other standard gauge locomotives and led the project that successfully recreated the Lynton & Barnstaple Railway's Baldwin 2-4-2T *Lyn.*

Interest in restoring an NG/G16 Garratt came after he accepted an invitation to have a footplate ride made by FR/WHR general manager and director Paul Lewin. He was, he says, instantly hooked and keen to be involved.

Working with FR/WHR chief mechanical engineer Jon Whalley, No. 130 was selected for restoration. In line with FR/WHR Company policy, the locomotive is owned by the company while the sponsor has paid for it to be returned to service. The advantage of this for the sponsor is that no VAT is incurred on expenditure incurred by a transport undertaking, while it would be if the work were carried out for an individual. The same applies to No. 87.

No. 130's power bogies, boiler cradle, bunker and water tank were delivered to Dinas on 26

A fine array of valves and gauges, seen in January 2021. (Peter Best Collection)

Obviously in steam, No. 130 stands at Dinas before making a light engine run to Tryfan Junction on 10 February 2021. (Peter Best Collection)

On 28 January 2021, a fire was lit to warm the boiler and check for leaks, a major step in the locomotive's restoration. The boiler was brought up to working pressure the next day. (Peter Best Collection)

A loaded run was made to Beddgelert on 14 April 2021, seen here crossing the Gwyrfai at Plas y Nant. (Chris Parry)

Above: *No. 130's sponsor, Peter Best, on the footplate of 'his' engine at Porthmadog on 26 April 2021. (Chris Parry)*

June 2015. Most of the work was carried out by railway employees at Dinas. The power bogies were overhauled at Boston Lodge and, later, the removable components were painted in the carriage workshop there.

The boiler was sent to the South Devon Railway for assessment. There it was realised that although it could be repaired it would be expensive to do so and the boiler would not have much life it in it. A new boiler, on the other hand, would not be that much more expensive and could be expected to last forty years or so. Accordingly, an order was placed with Northern Steam Engineering Ltd at Stockton on Tees, the sponsor considering the £160,000 cost to be exceptional value. Passing its out-of-frames steam test on 23 November 2018, it was delivered to Dinas in Jun 2019. The new boiler is not a copy of that originally fitted to No. 130 but is based on those fitted to the 1958 batch of NG/G16s, as an aid to future interchangeability if required.

Other major components replaced were the cab, the water tank and the coal bunker, the last two being manufactured by the Brunswick Ironworks in Caernarfon. No. 130 is painted in Burrell Plum, a rich maroon chosen by the sponsor; the same colour is used on the Canadian 'Royal Hudson' locomotive and has been adopted by the sponsor as his 'house colour.' It has also been applied to the S160 he had overhauled at the North Yorkshire Moors Railway and to the Barclay 0-4-0ST that he has installed as 'gate guardian' at his home in Gloucestershire.

The sponsor took a keen interest in No. 130s restoration and 'had fun' in acquiring parts in South Africa. He also visited Australia, where he exchanged Garratt stories with personnel at the Puffing Billy Railway.

The lockdowns that followed the outbreak of the Covid-19 pandemic in 2020 delayed completion by a year but on 26 April 2021 the project to restore No. 130 for use on the Welsh Highland Railway was brought to a successful conclusion with a triumphant run from Caernarfon to Porthmadog, a beaming sponsor on the footplate. The restoration had cost in excess of £900,000, resulting in both the most extensive and most expensive locomotive overhaul yet carried out on the FR/WHR, a credit to Peter Best and all the staff and contractors who contributed to it.

~ No.140 (Beyer, Peacock 7865, 1958) ~

Together with Nos.137 - 139, this locomotive was delivered new to Durban for service on the Natal branches of SAR in November 1958. Also, like these engines, it was initially fitted with brass cab-side plates reading (in this case) E140! The "E" plates were later replaced by plates showing just 140. Yet a third pair of plates was eventually cast to show the locomotive as NG140.

This locomotive was a long term stalwart of the Donnybrook line, remaining there until the closure of the section from Umzinto to Highflats in May 1985. No.140 appears to have received one of the last three steam workshop repairs at Pietermaritzburg (No.151, (Intermediate Repair, 01/84), No.140 (Heavy Repair, 03/84), No.131 (Heavy Repair, 09/84)). In 1985 No.140 was selected to haul a passenger service at the international "Expo-Durban 85" exhibition. At the request of the Railway Society of South Africa (RSSA) a 2km demonstration circuit of track was laid by South African Transport Services (SATS) in the Expo site. It provided the motive power for a demonstration train of carriages decorated with images of Smarties. No.140 was turned out in SAR black livery, although lettered RSSA. It was crewed by members of the local RSSA branch in Durban including the then Editor of *SA Rail*, Terry Hutson, together with his son and daughter.

In 1987 No.140 was bought from SATS by a consortium of Swiss enthusiasts - Robert Horlacher, Roger Waller (the 1990s designer and driving force behind the SLM rack tanks), Harald Nave and Urs Zullig. Arriving at Port Shepstone No.140 was immediately put into service with the Alfred County Railway as its boiler hydraulic certification did not expire until 13th March 1994. In its smart lined red livery (applied before it entered service on ACR) it became one of the locomotives (NG/G16s and a NG15) hauling the heavy timber trains from Harding to the interchange sidings at Port Shepstone. With the cessation of regular steam timber haulage from Harding No.140 became a performer on Banana Express duties from Port Shepstone to Izotsha or Paddock, still turned out in its smart red livery. These workings were no sinecure as the thrifty ACR management attached loaded timber cars to the return train from Paddock to Port Shepstone.

In 1991 two Class 91 diesel electric locomotives were leased from Spoornet. The operating pattern for steam and diesel traction then became as follows. On Sunday evenings the pair of class 91s would depart Port Shepstone with 26 empties for Harding. On Monday morning they would bring a double load back as far as Paddock before returning to Harding with empties previously left there by a steam train from Port Shepstone. Single-headed steam would then bring half the load down to the

Left: *When NG140 arrived new at Durban in November 1958 it was fitted with cab-side plates showing the running number "E140." These electric locomotive plates were carried for a few years in the early 1960s until correct steam plates were cast.* (Leith Paxton)

Above Left: *On 22nd January 1981, No.140 is caught at the servicing point at Highflats on the Umzinto to Donnybrook line. Having been detached from a Down freight it will return to Ixopo with an Up freight from Umzinto.* (Tony Leeson)

Above Right: *No.140 returns from Donnybrook towards its home sub-depot at Ixopo with its guard's van on 26th June 1984. Mjila is the point where the mixed gauge track from Donnybrook separates, the Cape gauge line being visible in the background.* (Tony Leeson)

Below: *No.140 received one of the last steam overhauls at the Pietermaritzburg workshops and is seen shortly afterwards at the Durban Expo85. The old railway station is prominent behind the Smarties decorated train which is negotiating the 2km of track circuit operated by the Railway Society of South Africa.* (Barry Tunnicliffe)

Above: *With the Umzinto to Donnybrook line closed No.140 was transferred to Port Shepstone where its long-dated boiler certificate was put to good use by the newly formed Alfred County Railway Co. General Manager Charlie Lewis is seen here in 1988, supervising the repaint into ACR red panelled livery.* (Tony Leeson)

Right: *On 4th August 1988 No.140 was receiving attention at the servicing point at Bongwana on the ACR. Note the customised ACR cab-side number plate and water car connected to the locomotive.* (Tony Leeson)

Below: *On an April day in 1989 No.140 heads the return Banana Express along the Indian Ocean coast towards Port Shepstone. In June 2008 this screw pile bridge was destroyed by flood waters after a storm.* (Charlie Lewis)

No.140 is seen passing Paddock station with a loaded timber train. (Terry Hutson, SA Rail collection)

Headed by No.140 a freight train descends the dramatic Wilson's cutting on 2nd May 1989. (Tony Leeson)

On 18th December 1990 No.140 takes on coal and water at the Port Shepstone servicing point before departing with a freight for Harding. (Tony Leeson)

No. 140 being assembled on arrival at Glan y Pwll on 7 April 1997. (Peter Johnson)

interchange sidings on Monday and the other half on Tuesday. Meanwhile, on Monday night, the two diesels would bring a full double load of timber (26 wagons, 600 tons gross) down from Harding in time for their inspection and servicing in Port Shepstone depot on Tuesday. On Tuesday nights the cycle would repeat itself with steam bringing down half the load plus the Banana Express coaches from Paddock on the Wednesday. The Banana Express ran on Wednesdays and Saturdays and when there were heavy passenger loadings this necessitated double heading by steam in order to clear the timber. This went on through the week which meant that steam was used on freight seven days per week until an additional (third) diesel was leased in 1998.

By 1994 No.140 required a major overhaul and was taken out of service. It was towed up the line, away from the salty seaside air, to storage at Classen's sidings at Paddock. Its Swiss owners then sold the locomotive to the FR Trust for the nominal sum of just £100. After its arrival in North Wales on 7 April 1997 those with a sharp eye would have noticed that the boiler mountings on this engine differed from those on No.138 and No.143. This was because No.140 carried a pre-war boiler (9061 of 1939). This boiler had originally carried the early pattern of boiler water top feed, steam manifold and safety valves. These, however, had been updated at a SAR overhaul to the post-war pattern when a new replacement outer firebox crown sheet was welded in. Although this change made the firebox arrangements the same as for post-war engines, the top feed clack valves remained positioned just ahead of the dome, rather than on the front ring of the barrel. The cab fittings for sight feed lubricators and the vacuum ejector were removed at the same time, the function of the former being replaced by the engine's buffer beam mounted mechanical lubricators, the ejector being transferred to the RHS of the firebox in front of the cab.

In North Wales No.140 was stored for some time in Glan-y-Pwll yard on the Ffestiniog Railway. With the approaching need for more WHR motive power the locomotive was moved to Dinas early in 2005, to allow overhaul to begin as a volunteer project. The locomotive was separated into its two component bogies, plus the boiler cradle and boiler, the latter being mounted on ambulance bogies. Work began on stripping down the bogies for overhaul, the tank and bunker being removed for separate repair. The front bogie was moved into the machine shop at Dinas. Much progress was made with the overhaul of pins, bushes and bearings. The cylinders and piston valves were re-bored.

Meanwhile, during 2005, the boiler and cradle stood on ambulance bogies in the headshunt of the running shed, the boiler cladding gradually being removed together with the tubes and superheater flues to allow a full boiler inspection. Later, in the Autumn, it was moved to the Goods Shed. During late Autumn and Winter the Wylfa team undertook the preparation of the boiler for detailed inspection. This involved de-scaling the barrel and firebox internally and de-scaling the whole externally and painting with heat resisting aluminium paint. The task proved arduous as the depth and hardness of internal scale suggested that water treatment had not been available in its previous life. West Midlands Group applied the top coat before the boiler was rolled out of the Goods Shed in time for the 2007 Beer Festival. With this task complete, a contract was let to carry out some repairs to the platework and see the boiler through to a successful steam test. The work was carried out by the LNWR Heritage workshops of the Waterman Railway Heritage Trust at Crewe. They also carried out the retubing and the fitting of new superheater flues.

In 2010 the boiler and cradle, together with the restored bogie, were transferred to Boston Lodge for completion of their repair. This was part of a plan for the rapid return of No.143 to steam after the expiry of its ten years boiler certificate in 2009. Following the completion of No.143 in 2011, No.140's boiler cradle carries the 1950-built boiler removed from No.143. The rear bogie of No.140 still stands in the open at Dinas awaiting overhaul whilst the front bogie runs under No.143. The hybrid nature of No.140, after these borrowings, does reflect the workshop practices of SAR, where a completely overhauled engine could be returned to traffic with many parts originally carried by other engines. It does mean however that the return to traffic of this one-time favourite engine of the Umzinto and Port Shepstone lines has a quite uncertain timescale.

Above: *After its purchase by the FR Trust for a nominal £100, No.140 was displayed at Glan y Pwll during the FR's May 1997 gala and was sometimes coupled up to No. 138, which was in steam. Much of the locomotive's boiler pipework and some fittings had been stolen during the time the locomotive had stood out of use at Port Shepstone.*
(Howard Wilson)

Above Inset: *The boiler data plate on the left hand side of the smokebox records that this is boiler No.9061, first set to work in 1939. Its most recent certification is recorded on the top row as in March 1984. The final stamp on the bottom row indicates that its expiry was in June 1994.* (David Payling)

Left: *The boiler and cradle of No.140 were under overhaul by volunteers at Dinas in October 2005. The dismantled locomotive is standing in the headshunt of the running shed.*
(David Payling)

~ *No.143 (Beyer, Peacock 7862, 1958)* ~

As the last steam engine constructed by Beyer, Peacock at Gorton No.143 is something of a celebrity. It was delivered new with Nos.141-2 to Port Elizabeth at the beginning of February 1959 for work on the 177 miles long Avontuur Branch of the Cape Midlands Section of SAR. As the final three of the seven NG/G16s ordered by the Tsumeb corporation, they had been built with cab-side number plates showing numbers TC10 – TC12. These were replaced by locally cast brass plates showing the correct SAR numbers before the engines entered traffic, the small Tsumeb ownership plates on the boiler cradles also being removed.

At Port Elizabeth, the fleet of twenty-one Class NG15 locomotives arrived from Usakos in South West Africa in early 1961. Their arrival prompted a redistribution of narrow gauge motive power and a number of NG/G13s and NG/G16s were transferred away to the Natal branches. On 30th January 1963, No.143 departed for Natal where it became something of a fixture on the Umzinto to Donnybrook line, remaining in service there until shortly before the line closed in 1986.

Work on the Umzinto to Donnybrook line was unlike that on the Avontuur Branch in that there was no heavy mineral traffic. An important source of its freight was from dairy farming, there being important creameries along the route. However, from the 1960s onwards, the main source of traffic was pulpwood for the Courtaulds dissolving pulp mill at Umkomaas. This was the business for

Above: *The works plate of NG/G16 No.143, the final steam locomotive built at Gorton by Beyer, Peacock.* (Tony Leeson)

Left: *No.143 had been in Africa fewer than four years when it was captured in this idyllic scene. It stands at Loerie in May 1962 in charge of service 628, the mixed train from Humewood Road in Port Elizabeth to Humansdorp some 69 miles away.* (Charlie Lewis)

Below: *No.143 heads a Westbound mixed train at Loerie in the early 1960s.* (Charlie Lewis)

Right: *Train No.628 from Humewood Road in Port Elizabeth draws into Thornhill, hauled by No.143. The Stone Tonum electric hadlight of the engine is prominent. In its 33 miles journey the train has already climbed some 700 ft above sea level.* (Charlie Lewis)

Inset left: *Two locomotives, NG/G16 No.143 and NG15 No.134, both now based on the Welsh Highland Railway, are seen at rest in the old servicing depot at Assegaaibos on the Avontuur branch in June 1962.* (Charlie Lewis)

Inset right: *The arrival of the 21 NG15s at Port Elizabeth displaced several Garratts, including No.143, to the Natal lines. In Natal No.143 was allocated to the Umzinto to Donnybrook line. The locomotive is seen here in its new home, out-shedded at Ixopo with No.113 on 4th July 1975.* (Tony Leeson)

which the 1967/8 batch of NG/G16s was ordered and the reason for the rebuilding of the Donnybrook line in the 1970s and 1980s in preparation for diesels. In the end the main beneficiaries of this rebuilding were the WHR and some RSA mines! There was also sugar cane traffic in the coastal areas. Further inland there was much timber traffic from the pine plantations which supplied the need for pit props in the mining areas around Johannesburg.

The Master Boiler Logbook for No.143's boiler has survived, starting from its last workshop repairs which were completed on 4th August 1977. With the decline in traffic on the Donnybrook line the engine was transferred to Port Shepstone in the mid-1980s. Here it spent the last year or two of the line's SAR life hauling timber trains from Harding together with the traffic in agricultural produce. The boiler hydraulic test certificate expired on 3rd August 1986. This was perhaps the main reason why, when the Alfred County Railway Co. commenced operations in Port Shepstone, No.143 remained out of use, eventually being transferred to storage at Paddock (Classen's sidings) in 1992.

Despite its poor mechanical and boiler condition in 1994, No.143 was chosen for refurbishment for service on the WHR. This was because of its historical importance as the last Beyer, Peacock steam locomotive and the last Beyer, Peacock Garratt to be built. It was moved early in 1995 from Paddock for overhaul at Port Shepstone. The work was not complete in time for the Ffestiniog Travel special train from Port Shepstone to Harding, its place in the double header being taken by No.155, Phil Girdlestone's second NG/G16A producer gas combustion rebuild. After completion of its overhaul in the early Autumn of 1996, when it double headed an acceptance trial train with No.138, it was shipped to North Wales, arriving in January 1997.

Unfortunately, it was found that further mechanical and boiler work would be required before

Above Left: *On 5th September 1980 No.143 heads a mixed freight train near Kenterton on the Umzinto branch of SAR in Natal.* (Neville Fields)

Above Right: *With the rundown of the Umzinto line No.143 was transferred to Port Shepstone in the mid-1980s. It is seen here at the Izingolweni servicing point on 24th July 1986. The brown uniformed guard is about to accept the token for the next block section.* (Tony Leeson)

Right: *This view of the cab of No.143 was taken at Umzinto on 2nd April 1972. Unlike Natal's Nos.137-140, the three NG /G16s allocated to Port Elizabeth in 1958-9 had not been mistakenly given "E" plates.* (Terry Hutson, SA Rail collection)

Below: *While No.143 was being serviced at Izingolweni on 24th July 1986 the local police arrived. They asked the engine crew to help by burning some sacks of confiscated illegal marijuana (dagga)! The photograph shows the sacks about to disappear into the fireboxes of Nos.126 and 143.* (Tony Leeson)

Above: *No. 143's cradle and boiler, showing the effect of sea transport as deck cargo, in the Glan y Pwll carriage shed on 15 January 1997.* (Peter Johnson)

Left: *No. 143's boiler at Riley & Son (E) Ltd's works, then at Bury, Lancashire, on 1 August 1997.* (Peter Johnson)

Left: *No. 143's smokebox and front tube plate.* (Peter Johnson)

Above: *A close-up of No. 143's boiler shell, showing studs, plugs and rivets that have been replaced.* (Peter Johnson)

Right: *The boiler back in the frames and restoration of No. 143 approaching completion at Dinas on 2 July 1998.* (Peter Johnson)

Below: *It moves! With the drain cocks open, No. 143 moves under its own steam for the first time in Wales, 17 September 1998.* (Peter Johnson)

Above: *The first appearance of two Garratts at Caernarfon occurred on 18 September 1998. With the locos double-heading, the train was too long for the loop, causing the locos to be separated as shown.*
(Peter Johnson)

Left: *Seen at Dinas on 29 September 1998, the broken flange on No. 143's super-heater header that caused the loco to be withdrawn a few weeks after its launch earlier in the month. A replacement was obtained from South Africa.*
(Peter Johnson)

Above: *In North Wales both Garratts were in steam for the WHR's 1998 Gala weekend of 19-20th September. Afterwards, No.143 had to return to the workshop for further attention to its superheater, before entry into regular service.* (Tony Martin)

Left: *The Superpower weekend of 2003 enjoyed good weather. On 13th September No.143 approaches the high Glanrafon bridge with a Caernarfon-bound train. Under a clear sky, the waste tips of Glanrafon slate quarry form the background.* (Roy Woods)

Below: *The camera of Peter Treloar caught No.143 at the old water tank siding at Caernarfon on 14th September 2002. The paintwork, number plates, stainless steel boiler bands and polished copper and brass pipework of the engine had been restored to be as close as possible to its appearance in SAR service.* (Peter Treloar)

No.143 restarts its train from Hendy Crossing. All trains were obliged to stop here momentarily owing to the poor sight lines for both rail and road users. Regulations meant that, in this view, at least twelve notices to road users can be seen! (David Payling)

Top right: *Rhyd Ddu was journey's end in May 2004 and trains used the Down line of the platform. There was no water tank at the Caernarfon end of the short platform and no shelter from the weather!* (David Payling)

Right: *The 10.00 train stands at Dinas awaiting the guard's Right Away. This first train of the day customarily started its journey down to Caernarfon from the Up platform.* (David Payling)

Above: *The Afon Gwrfai bridge at Plas-y-Nant had been strengthened with additional waybeams to support the weight of the new trains. No.143 comes cautiously round the very sharp curve on to the bridge on 4th May 2004.* (David Payling)

Above: *The gorse is in flower on 8th April 2009 as No.143 passes under the main road bridge at Castell Cidwm on its way to Rhyd Ddu. The blue background to the cab-side number plate was used in SAR days in Natal to denote an engine based on the Umzinto line.*
(David Payling)

Above inset: *No.143 rolls down the gradient through Coed Mawr as it approaches Meillionen Halt for Beddgelert's large camping site. Trains heading up the gradient face a difficult re-start on the 1 in 40 if a stop is required at this halt. On No.143 the small triangular flag visible above the line of the front of the tank is an indication to the driver as to whether the steam operated sanding valves are open or shut.*
(David Payling)

Left: *The guard is checking that the carriage doors are secure as the train prepares to depart from Rhyd Ddu for Beddelert and Hafod-y-Llyn on 20th August 2009.*
(David Payling)

the locomotive boiler could be certified and insured for service in the UK. This was carried out by Riley & Son (E) Ltd of Bury. The locomotive entered traffic at the Enthusiasts' Weekend in September 1998. Since then it has proved itself to be a strong steamer and very reliable in service. Because of its historical significance it was decided that No.143 should retain its SAR identity and appearance. It thus retained its glossy black SAR livery with bright stainless steel boiler bands together with polished brass boiler pipe-work. It retained its SAR cab-side number plates. On the Umzinto line these had been embellished with a blue painted background to the central area around the number.

With the expiry of its boiler certificate in 2009 the locomotive was taken out of traffic for overhaul after sharing haulage of the Christmas and New Year special trains. With the line about to be opened to passenger trains from end to end in the 2010 season it was of great operational importance to have the

Right: *The 2009 season was the last for No.143 before its 10-yearly major overhaul. By this time the locomotive had amassed many miles in service and on 19th September, during Superpower weekend, it experienced a rare mechanical failure and had to be detached from its train at Beddgelert. Here it is seen in the short Up siding awaiting rescue.* (Roy Woods)

Below left: *At Dinas, in September 2009, the boiler taken from No.140 was awaiting transport to the LNWR workshops at Crewe. The flange for the boiler water feed valves can be seen close to the dome front. This was characteristic of pre-war NG/G13 and NG/G16 boilers. The line of the weld where the original firebox crown had been replaced by a post-war top can be seen on the firebox side. Volunteers at Dinas had prepared the boiler by removal of all tubes and flues, followed by the arduous task of removing many years of lime scale.* (David Payling)

Below right: *At Crewe the boiler from No.140 was repaired, re-tubed and steam tested and certificated for the next ten years. By 19th April 2010, the boiler was undergoing its final live steam test under the supervision of the FR's boiler inspector, Mr Errol Jones, and one of the apprentices.* (Jon Whalley)

engine back in traffic at the earliest opportunity. To that end the 1939 boiler from No.140, which had been stripped and scaled by Wylfa Power Station volunteers, was sent to the LNWR workshop at Crewe for repairs to the backhead, foundation ring and the re-riveting of parts of the boiler barrel. At the same time the boiler tubes and superheater flues were fitted and the completed boiler steam tested. After its return in mid-2010 the new superheater elements were fitted in the erecting shop at Boston Lodge. At the same time the locomotive was converted from oil burning to coal. This reflected the great escalation in fuel oil costs of the previous few years. In 2010 the fuel oil firing on No.138 had cost an average of £12.14 per mile, whilst the coal fired No.87 had cost £4.12 per mile, a difference of a factor of three!

The frames and cylinders of one of the bogies of No.140 were transferred to Boston Lodge and the bogie completed from the fittings taken from No.143's bogie. The other bogie from No.143 received a complete overhaul. To complete the work the valve setting of all four cylinders was undertaken under the leadership of contractor, Llyr ap Iolo. With extensive corrosion to the front water tank, a new welded fabrication was ordered from the Brunswick Ironworks in Caernarfon. The rear bunker also was newly fabricated at Boston Lodge, being adapted for coal storage rather than oil. The locomotive was lit up on 11th June 2011 with a small wood fire to dry the new brick arch in the firebox. Testing began during the following week and the locomotive entered full normal service at the end of July. The benefit of the work on the valve settings immediately became obvious with both water and coal consumption proving remarkably economical in comparison with other engines. Also, the thorough overhaul of the power bogies has led to a very quiet, smooth running engine in comparison with the other two NG/G16s.

Under overhaul as the revised edition is prepared for publication, No. 143 will be returned to service with No. 129's boiler, a new smiokebox and the power units formerly used by No. 138.

On 11th June 2011 No.143 emerged from its major overhaul at Boston Lodge. The engine had been repainted in British Railways steam locomotive green with orange lining against a black background. The new steam sanding gear is visible coupled to the bottom flange of the sand boxes on the water tank front. (Andrew Thomas)

Top: *After last minute adjustments No.143 was out on the line under test with Works Manager Tony Williams at the controls. Note the spark-proofing around the ash pan.* (Andrew Thomas)

Left above: *Watched by a small crowd of onlookers, No.143 cautiously ventures onto the WHR on its first running-in turn on 21st June 2011.* (Chris Parry)

Left: *True Superpower! On the WHR's Gala weekend of 2011 No.143 triple heads with sister engines, Nos.87 and 138 towards Ynysfor and Pont Croesor on 11th September.* (Chris Parry)

- IX -
GARRATTS FROM THE SHARP END

~ *John Hancock, Driver on the Severn Valley Railway* ~

Readers may be wondering how a Severn Valley Railway driver ended up writing about Garratts on the Welsh Highland Railway? Well, the answer is that a conversation one day with my friend and fireman, Colin Astbury, led a few weeks later to my introduction to Paul Lewin, General Manager of arguably the finest narrow gauge heritage railway on the planet. When we first met, I was in the pit at Bewdley on the Severn Valley Railway, checking and oiling Stanier Mogul No. 42968 when Paul reached between the wheels to shake my oily paw. It was in 2008, I think, and I believe it's safe to say we "Got On;" acquaintance became friendship and led to a reciprocal invitation.

Thus, at 0830hrs on Friday, 4th July 2008, Colin and I found ourselves gazing at the prototype Garratt, K1, brewing up at Dinas depot, as Paul and his fireman, Aaron, busied themselves with preparation duties. We also got a chance to check out the impressive, elegant bulk of NG/G16 No.138 which was undergoing maintenance, having just had a power unit swap.

One of the first tasks of the day is lighting up. The fireman uses a paraffin-soaked rag to light a stack of wood and small coals in the firebox of No.87. His reserve supply of scrap wood lies on the cab floor.
(David Payling)

Shortly afterwards, Paul threw some cleaning rags at us and, taking the hint, we set about K1 which was still in semi-matt black, not yet fully lined out. With preparations and cleaning complete, Paul took us out of the depot and on to our train in Dinas station. Even with four of us in the cab, there was still room to move. I was then instructed to take the regulator for our run to Caernarfon. Paul mentioned that the engine would be working initially on one end only, the high pressure end, and not to worry if it slips. If it did, this would expedite steam getting to the low pressure cylinders which in turn would then join the party.

With a "Rightaway!" from Paul, I opened the regulator and K1 eased our train away without any drama. We had seven vehicles including one bicycle wagon, one open sided coach, four saloon coaches and one Pullman, "Bodysgallen." The regulator was easy to move and the exhaust sounded normal for a short while. It then developed extra beats as the low pressure engine kicked in, before synchronising and sounding normal again. I didn't have much time to

Above: *Coal firing on the WHR brought the need for coaling facilities at Dinas. At first they were quite rudimentary and, on 29th April 2008, K1 is seen receiving a wheelbarrow load of coal. By this time a taller set of coal rails had been made to allow sufficient to be carried.* (John Ellis Williams)

get used to it as, shortly after passing the carriage shed, we commenced the descent to Caernarfon at 1 in 60. The regulator was closed and I kept the train in check with the vacuum brake, the "feel" of the train being identical to that of a Severn Valley train.

Any experienced footplate man and, after thirty years on Severn Valley footplates, I guess I qualify, is quickly at home on a different engine. Once you've sorted out where the injector valves (water & steam), the blower and the dampers are, you're in your comfort zone. It is blindingly obvious where the regulator and brake are and again, once you've been briefed on any bits you're unaware of, such as an independent steam brake, you're most of the way there. Any driver automatically scans water level and steam pressure at regular intervals, alternating this with checking the road ahead.

K1 has an addition not normally found on British main line steam engines, other than the big and fast ones and the later B.R. Standard classes, a steam chest pressure gauge. This tells you what is actually going into the cylinders and proves incredibly useful, Paul using it to advise me on train handling throughout this trip and subsequent ones on the big Garratts, which also have these gauges.

Though K1 has a slightly old fashioned appearance, hardly surprising considering its birth date, it was smooth riding and a complete sweetheart to drive, fine control being easily achieved by small adjustments of the regulator. In this way, by monitoring the steam chest gauge, an extra 10 or 20lbs on the gauge picks the train up following a change of gradient, maybe after a dive under a bridge where the footings have had to be deepened to allow Garratts inside the structure gauge. Equally, closing the regulator, or just leaving a "breath" of drifting steam on, maintains progress over the easier sections.

This was my first trip over the Welsh Highland Railway and, as such, required enormous concentration as it is a complex "road." As a result I didn't absorb as much of K1 as I would

Sanding of the rails is required in poor weather conditions to allow trains to climb the 1 in 40 gradients of the WHR. A special grade of gritty sand is essential, combined with automatic steam powered delivery to the rails. (David Payling)

Above: *Oiling round the motion is a significant task on a NG/G16, the engine having four sets of Walschaert's valve gear, each with its many pins and bushes to lubricate. The cork protecting each joint must be released and the cavity filled with oil as the driver makes his morning inspection.* (John Dobson)

have liked, concentrating on following Paul's instructions, in order to keep to time and obey the numerous speed restrictions. I absorbed enough, however, to know I was becoming very fond of the engine. I'd first made its acquaintance in 1966, on an escorted trip round Boston Lodge as part of a geography field trip arranged by my grammar school. It was tucked round the back of a shed and obviously far too big to work on the Ffestiniog Railway.

Later that year (2008 now -time jump, keep up!) Paul contacted me to say he had been rostered to drive on the WHR on 29th and 30th December, presumably because no-one else was available or willing. Did I fancy a trip? I certainly did and, after a bit of domestic negotiation, booked my wife and myself into the Seiont Manor Hotel for a post-Christmas break.

The weather was bitterly cold and had been for a couple of days. It was the sort of cold that leaves everywhere rimed with frost which sparkled in crystal clear sunshine and rendered the spectacular scenery achingly beautiful. Dinas depot was in shadow and predictably cold, but NG/G16 No.143 was brewing up and, like all steam engines, creating its own microclimate. Believe me, all loco crews appreciate the warmth which surrounds an engine in steam when the weather is cold. Paul was oiling round the motion, so I kept out of his way and walked round, checking the beast out.

The Garratts are impressive close up. In size and power they are often compared with the ex-LMS Ivatt Class 2 locomotives. It should be emphasised that this is a very broad brush comparison. Tractive effort, which is a mathematical expression involving wheel diameter, cylinder dimensions and steam pressure, gives figures of 17,410lb. for the Ivatt against 21,360lb. for the Garratt. This would imply that the Garratt is more powerful than the Ivatt. However this takes no account of reality.

The Ivatt 2s were well known to be fleet of foot, the tender engines recorded at speeds in excess of 70mph and the tank versions being reported, by respected timers, in the high 80s, right up to the last two years of steam on British Railways. I have fired and driven them on many occasions and can confirm they will pick up their skirts and go, if asked. An NG/G16 would have flown to bits long before those speeds were approached. Likewise the Ivatt would undoubtedly struggle with a load that the Garratt, with its much smaller wheels, would handle with ease.

The weights are broadly comparable: a Garratt in working order being around 62 tons and an Ivatt 2 tank, (the most appropriate comparison as it, too, carries its coal and water over the wheels) weighing in at 63 tons 5 cwt. I was fortunate to land a night

Left: *Before the journey can begin there is the delicate task of coupling up to be carried out. Care is required to avoid a jolt to passengers at the front of the train!* (David Payling)

turn on 41241 on a Severn Valley Autumn Steam Gala a couple of years ago and was very sad to part with it. This beautifully restored Ivatt Class 2 tank normally lives at the Keighley and Worth Valley Railway.

The Ivatt Class 2s were designed and built for branch passenger and trip goods work and they are excellent and comfortable to work on. I have fired and driven them on eight coach trains (279 tons tare) and on nine, when an observation saloon has been added. They will do the job on the Severn Valley's ruling

Above: *The driver of the train arriving at Waunfawr from Rhyd Ddu exchanges the token for that block section for the token to Dinas. The Rhyd Ddu token is being taken by the fireman of the Up train, out of view on the other platform, which has just arrived from Dinas. The guards of the two trains watch the action!* (David Payling)

gradients of 1 in 100, but it's hard work. The engine is well outside its comfort zone and has to be leathered. On four coaches, later on during that same night shift, Ivatt tender engine No.46443 was like a gazelle by comparison and it was a blissful run....... The ride on the tender engines could best be described as "lively!"

Returning from the "Broad Gauge" to Dinas; as Paul took the train down to Caernarfon, I remember remarking that we might have fun coming back as the railhead looked to be fouled. As a long time SVR permanent way man, I have seen it before. The ride on the Garratt was suspiciously smooth and quiet. On the regulator from Caernarfon, I eased us out of the station and No.143 got quietly into its stride, the exhaust resounding satisfyingly from the trees and huge volumes of steam condensing in the bitterly cold air. All went well for a couple of minutes. Then came the first slip, quickly corrected, then another and another until, before long, we slipped to a stand. Despite all my experience, I was unable to re-start the train. Paul took over, but fared little better and, eventually, we blew the train brakes down and got off to examine the track.

Railhead conditions were dreadful. "Leaves on the line" is a familiar phrase to anyone who uses trains, but few realise just how bad this can be. In our case, we had a mix of crushed leaves and ice adhering to the railhead. The leaf mulch causes the wheels to lose contact with the rail, initially causing them to spin, as the coefficient of friction drops below the value needed to sustain adhesion. Then Act 2 opens as the spinning wheels generate heat and melt the ice, forming a perfect slurry: adhesion-wise, we were toast. We ended up hand sanding the rails for about 150 yards, using Styrofoam cups and the sand which was normally fed into the firebox at intervals to clean the tubes of oil fired No.143.

Paul had a conversation with one of the locals, who informed him that some trains used to stick in the same spot when the line was still standard gauge, so it's not just us!

Finally, using all of his considerable skill and experience, Paul got us away and we made it into Dinas. I then took over for the rest of the trip to Rhyd Ddu and back and, although there was some more slipping here and there, the journey was fine, the Garratt riding smoothly and master of its job. Like K1, it is easy and comfortable to drive, the regulator easy to adjust to maintain your chosen steam chest pressure. The Gresham and Craven brake, although different from what I am used to, had the same effect as those on a Severn Valley train.

That particular lesson was not lost on Paul and, the following year, a programme of tree cutting on that section was instituted to alleviate the problem. The incident also serves to highlight the difficulties in achieving balance in locomotive design. The NG/G16s were designed to run in hot, dry, South Africa and provide significant power over lightly laid tracks. I doubt it was envisaged that they would end up lugging heavy passenger trains on steep gradients in wet, windswept, leafy Wales! An Ivatt 2 tank spreads its 63+ tons over five axles; a Garratt over ten, so the Ivatt is putting over 12 tons on each axle, against the Garratt's 6.2 tons.

A double Fairlie, by way of comparison, is putting 6.75 tons on each axle. I had a run on *Earl of Merioneth* the day before my run on K1 and was mightily impressed. We were only pulling eight coaches and the engine was driven entirely in first valve. Nigel Burbidge, the driver, informed me that second valve was only needed if the Fairlies had twelve on. The engine was the complete master of the job and acceleration was impressive, being rapidly up to line speed on the Cob, which seemed a lot faster than the 20mph it was. I took over at Tan-y-Bwlch, where the rain was coming down in stair rods! Despite Nigel warning me that the start from TyB could be tricky in these conditions, we got away without slipping and I found the engine very sure footed all the way to Blaenau Ffestiniog.

That's my only drive on a double engine so far, but I'm looking forward to the next one. My other two forays on the Ffestiniog have both been on the Penrhyn "ladies," *Blanche* and *Linda*. I can best describe this as just the greatest fun. I drove *Linda* this summer, when she was in "cabriolet convertible" mode with the cab back sheet under repair. It started to rain at Blaenau Ffestiniog (spot the developing theme here), from where we were tender first and, by the time I got to Boston Lodge halt, I didn't think I could get any wetter. Then we ran out on to the Cob and I felt the full benefit of the storm...............

In 2009 I was presented with an "opportunity" to fire NG/G16 No.87, as a result of a benign conspiracy between the same P Lewin, Esq, and his fireman, James Hamlin, who handed me the shovel at Caernarfon with the words, "We thought you'd like to have a go." As he walked off to assist Paul with filling the tank I enquired, "How long have we got?" to his departing back and caught the words, "Five minutes!" flung breezily over the shoulder. Mates, eh?

The briefing (emphasis on brief) consisted of, "It seems to like a U-shaped fire, thick in the back corners and under the door and sloping down at the sides. Leave it thin in the centre and at the front, but don't let any holes appear by the front corners."

I started shovelling. The shovel, virtually identical to my own short-handled tank engine shovel, felt very comfortable as I baled six into the back left-hand corner, then six more into the right. Realising the 'box' was deeper than it looked, I slung another four into each corner, until I could see the coal, then eight or nine under the door, followed by three or four down each side, nudging the blower on a bit more to keep the smoke down. By this time, Paul and James had finished topping up the tank and were backing on to the train. I paused for breath, thinking, "B----- hell, I don't put this many on a Black Five!" (big "broad gauge" mixed traffic 4-6-0. Nothing to get excited about -not articulated).

As I was ladling a couple more just under the door to make a little "tump" (or possibly "twmp," since we were in Wales) in order to cut down the radiance from the surprisingly large firehole Paul, who was watching the guard, called "Rightaway!" Then, as he opened the regulator, observed helpfully "Your overalls are about to catch fire, John." As I danced a little to keep the hot cloth from my leg, I reflected on another Garratt character trait; it's a large fire hole and you can't get far enough away from it sometimes. It's similar to the ex-Great Western pannier tanks and other engines with confined cabs – and it's why enginemen wear overalls. It's not to keep clean, it's to protect you from the heat!

If you've ever been on the footplate and maybe tried your hand at throwing a couple of shovels on, you're probably wondering what the problem is. Well, in that case, it isn't a problem but, when the engine is working hard, that fire is white-hot, the temperature 2000-3,500 degrees (Fahrenheit – none of your metric nonsense!) – hot enough to produce ultraviolet light. You can't stay in front of it for more than a second or two, which is a problem when you've got to keep shovelling.

As the train cleared the station, Paul opened up to some purpose and the Garratt, still with only seven coaches on, marched effortlessly up the gradient, its exhaust providing some entertainment for walkers on the adjacent Lôn Eifion footpath. I had had the injector on a couple of times as the needle approached the red line but, a couple of miles out, I ran out of space in the boiler and the engine blew off spectacularly. What can I say? Sometimes you just can't get the staff.....

By the time we reached Dinas I had got a grip of the job and managed to keep us in pretty good shape up to Rhyd Ddu. This was the third time I'd done the run and some of it was looking familiar. I was also becoming comfortable with the engine; it doesn't take long for any experienced footplate man to get an idea of what the machine is doing; they talk to you. It's the same when Paul and other Ffestiniog men have visited me at the Valley. Knowing the "road" is the difficult part; once you know what is ahead of

The WHR currently uses the "staff and ticket" system to control traffic on the single line. Before a train can proceed the fireman takes the token for the next Section, with permission from the Controller. It must then be shown to both guard and driver, with the inscription read out aloud. (David Payling)

The Waunfawr stop comes after the climb from Caernarfon to Dinas at 1 in 60 and on from Dinas to Tryfan Junction at 1 in 40. Much steam will have been used, so "putting the bag in" at Waunfawr is an essential task for the crew. (David Payling)

you, you can put the engine right for the job.

Apart from a bit of "fine tuning" with the shovel, occasional and judicious use of the injector and damper as necessary, the journey to Rhyd Ddu passed uneventfully. It gave me the chance to take in some of the stunning scenery and do a bit of route learning. I also noticed that, standing with your back to the bunker, the shovelling plate would nudge you in the back of your legs, as the rear power unit negotiated the curves, the rigid boiler and cab unit ploughing its own furrow.

Pulling into Rhyd Ddu, the limit of my travels to that time, anticipation was tying a small knot in my stomach –I was seriously looking forward to the next bit. Paul and James pronounced themselves satisfied with the fire and the water level in the boiler and we were away again. In a couple of minutes we had climbed serenely to the summit at Pitt's Head and were diving down the 1 in 40 into Beddgelert Forest, my eyes glued to the water gauge. I was gratified to see it still showing a comfortable quarter to a third of a glass, even under braking. Braking is a continuous feature of this section, in this direction, in order to maintain speed and control. This causes the water in the boiler to move forward which carries the risk of uncovering the firebox crown, unless you have plenty in which, fortunately, I did.

Entering Beddgelert, I was mentally ticking off another dream come true. I observed as Paul brought the train to a stand, before destroying the train vacuum to zero, as well as the engine brake. For good measure, the reverser was wound into full back gear and the cylinder drain cocks shut. This meant that any leakage of steam through the regulator would be trapped in the cylinders and act to prevent the train moving. With a continuous 1 in 40 grade through the station, it pays to take every possible precaution against a runaway and seemed eminently sensible to me. Paul also mentioned that the engine is never left unattended at Beddgelert.

With a blast on that glorious chime whistle we were off again, into the rocky, black maw of Goat Tunnel, descending towards the matchless beauty of the Aberglaslyn Pass. As we rumbled across Bryn-y-Felin bridge, I had another one of those flashback moments to the time when I first walked across the original bridge 45 years ago, idly daydreaming of what it would be like to ride across it on a train.

I continued to drink in the views as we travelled through the Pass; the Afon Glaslyn, swollen a little by the rain earlier in the week, tumbling and chuckling alongside, breaking into white water here and there, around the numerous rocks scattered along its bed. I have followed the construction websites avidly over the last few years and eagerly studied the photographs but nothing prepares you for the real thing. This is truly breathtaking, world class scenery, owing nothing to anywhere else on

Coal firing also requires attention to the ashpan. K1 is seen here receiving attention in mid-journey on 29th April 2008. (John Ellis Williams)

the planet and we on the engine, and our passengers in the train behind, had the best view of it. From the road it's OK but, compared to the train, it's like being on the reverse of a picture postcard.

James had advised me that, to prepare for the return run, I would have to start sorting the fire as we left the dripping, Stygian gloom of the long tunnel (T4), the run round at Hafod-y-Llyn being decidedly brief. Obediently, I began shovelling and continued, missing Cwm Bychan and Nantmor Bank completely until, in a surprisingly short time, we had come to a stand at Hafod.

I carried on shovelling steadily as Paul and James ran the engine round the train, closing the fire doors occasionally to prevent self-combustion. I had to root for the coal a little, the supply having been depleted somewhat by my earlier efforts. The damper was wide open and the blower on quite hard to warm up the firebox and the brick arch before the work to come. The radiance from the fire hole was intense with the doors open and I could not stand in front of it for more than a few seconds.

"Rightaway" again and we were off, accelerating rapidly to the ski jump that is Nantmor Bank and soaring up it to my delight, a perfect grey exhaust and the needle on the red line. I was able to appreciate the scenery a bit more as we crossed over the new road bridge and hammered through Cwm Bychan into the black hole of T4 once again. We didn't dawdle through here as, although we were bunker first and thus in front of our exhaust, we were conscious that our passengers would be "getting the benefit," clearances between train and tunnel wall being on the tight side.

My next memory is of the stop at Beddgelert, where we had to run in under power, due to the adverse gradient, and shut off just in time to stop at the column to take water. While Paul and James were thus engaged, I added another few shovels to the incandescent mass inside the doors, only avoiding setting fire to myself by closing the doors between shovels.

The rest of the trip to the summit was just euphoric, amongst the finest I have ever experienced

Journey's End, 1. Under their teacher's watchful eye, young passengers take the opportunity to have a closer look at the cab controls of a Beyer-Garratt in May 2004. (David Payling)

on any steam engine, anywhere. I listened, entranced, to that beautiful crisp Lempor exhaust echoing from the trees, as No.87 forged onwards and upwards, without hesitation, injector on all the way, just holding the safety valves shut. My spirits were soaring, my body suffused with that visceral feeling that a steam engine imparts when all is sound and fury. It soars again as I type, the memory vivid and enduring. It's safe to say I was pretty happy by the time we got into Rhyd Ddu, from where I took over the regulator for the run back to Caernarfon.

After the carriages have been stored in the North Yard shed at Dinas, the footplate crew put the engine to bed in the running shed in the South Yard. Fireman Cedric Lodge (left) and driver Tony Williams have just completed the disposal of No.143 and pause a moment for the camera on 12th September 2002. (David Payling)

Journey's End, 2. There may be time during the layover for the footplate crew to take a moment to enjoy bacon and eggs from the fireman's shovel. (John Ellis Williams)

Since that trip I have had a couple more which have extended my experience almost all the way through to Porthmadog. Apparently there are one or two legal niceties which mean that there has to be a properly licensed WHR driver in charge over the tramway bits. From Hafod-y-Llyn the terrain is largely flat over the Traeth and the Garratts lope along comfortably at line speed with 10 – 25lbs on the clock and the lever well up the rack, proper expansive working. It's a complete contrast to the gut wrenching excitement of the hilly bits, but is another example of how well suited the Garratts are to the work.

This, then, is the reality of life on a NG/G16 Garratt, a free-steaming, pleasant-riding engine which is master of its job, impressive to look at and comfortable to work on. They weren't designed to drag trains up a wet hillside in Wales, yet they do so admirably, surely a tribute to the soundness of the design. The adhesion problems are being overcome; a combination of automatic steam sanding, plus judicious vegetation removal, is sorting out the job.

As a solution to the Welsh Highland's enviable problems of heavy loadings, tight curves and fierce gradients they are, quite simply, inspirational. I am a fan!

- X -
Development of the Kalahari NG15 Locomotive

The origins of the design for the SAR Class NG15 locomotive lay not in the CME's Department at Pretoria, but in the German colony of South West Africa (Namibia, since independence from South Africa in 1990). This territory was the location of the Otavi Railway, opened throughout in 1906 (see railway maps at the end of the book). A remarkable 356 miles long, the 24in. gauge line (more correctly 600mm gauge, as the German colonial lines followed the metric system) had been built early in the colonial period by the Otavi Minen und Eisenbahn Gesellschaft. This company had been set up to exploit the mineral riches discovered in the Tsumeb region of the interior of the territory. The railway had been surveyed and built by the German contractor Arthur Koppel. Starting from the coast at Swakopmund it crossed the 90 miles wide waterless Namib desert. Most of this was at a steady climb of 1 in 60, a little steeper in average gradient than the Ffestiniog Railway. At Usakos (93¾ miles) it reached a more hospitable terrain and it was here that the headquarters and workshops of the railway were built. Shortly beyond Usakos the railway branched with a line heading southwards via Karibib to Windhoek, the state capital. The line to the mines at Tsumeb continued North Easterly, at first through scrubland, and then through terrain which became progressively more fertile and suited to farming. Steady climbing continued beyond Usakos for a further 80 miles before the line reached the African plateau. For the rest of the journey the going became much easier.

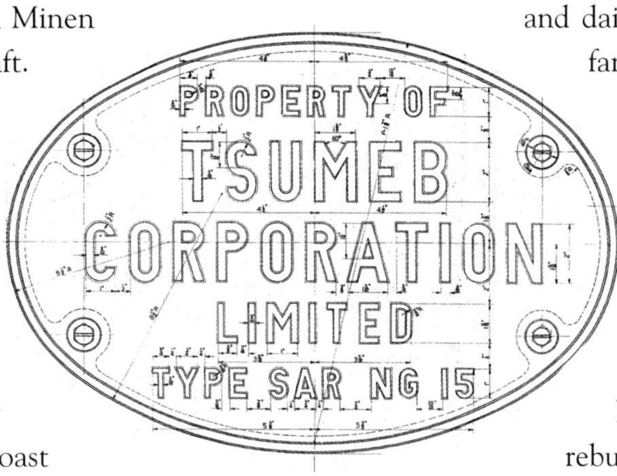

The Otavi Railway settled down to what proved to be 54 years of narrow gauge service to South West Africa (SWA). Its main traffic was of course the minerals and refined metals from the rich lodes around Tsumeb down to the ships at Swakopmund. Added to this was a lucrative traffic in farm and dairy products from the inland farming areas, plus a passenger traffic of tribesmen from the Ovambo lands in the North on their way to work in the diamond fields around Elizabeth Bay in the South. During the First World War the Namib desert section was rebuilt to the Cape gauge (see Section 2, below). After this, all mineral and other goods had to be transhipped at the break of gauge at Usakos. This labour intensive procedure was never automated and added to the difficulty and costs of working the line.

To this day South West Africa remains thinly populated. Towns were few and far between. The geology of the region was limestone and it was these two features of the terrain that set the direction for motive power development on the Otavi. Curvature of the line was not the important issue that it was for the narrow gauge lines in Natal and the Cape.

Possibly for this reason, articulation of locomotives did not become an established design feature. In South West Africa the challenge for locomotives was more importantly that they should be capable of running the long distances between water and fuel stops which were generally located at centres of population. Of equal importance was that they should be sufficiently powerful to be able to haul an economic load of minerals on their journey to the port. In the early days of the line the limestone hardness of the water taken from boreholes proved to have a very deleterious effect on the boilers and fireboxes which became heavily scaled. According to some reports, workshop attention to boilers was routinely required after only a few weeks of service! Water treatment plant was soon installed at key locations.

~ 1. *The Early Tank Engine Classes* ~

For the opening in 1906 the Otavi Railway was equipped with medium powered tank engines supplied by Jung and by Orenstein and Koppel. To give them an adequate range of operation they were soon equipped with double ended bogie tenders, some being supplied by Orenstein and Koppel, and some built locally at Usakos. The initial locomotives were rapidly followed by larger 0-6-2T locomotives from Henschel, identified as Class Hb. Fifteen were built between 1905 and 1908 (Nos.51-65) and were employed on mixed traffic or passenger services. Inspection of the works photograph shows them to have been built with a radial truck axle beneath the cab rather than a Bissell truck. Feed water pumps on the tank top were brought into use when weather conditions made the water in the tanks too warm for the injectors to be reliable. The Hb engines, too, ran semi-permanently coupled to bogie tenders carrying both water and extra coal.

The Henschel works photograph of Otavi Railway Class Hb locomotive No.63.
(NGRS Archive)

Above: *The long distances between water points soon necessitated the semi-permanent coupling of an auxiliary tender (and an additional crew man) to the Hb engines.* (NGRS Archive)

Left: *A member of Class Hb, No.56, survives in Namibia, together with its auxiliary tender and representative rolling stock. The location is the Old Fort, Robert Mugabe Avenue, Windhoek.* (David Payling)

~ 2. The 2-8-2 Tender Freight Engines, Class NG5 ~

The practice of operating the Otavi's tank engines effectively as tender engines was recognised and incorporated into the design of the next locomotives. These were three 2-8-2 tender engines intended for freight work and were supplied by Henschel in 1912 as Class Hd (Nos. 40 - 42). They were equipped with a generous grate and a fine free steaming boiler whose effectiveness was enhanced by a large two row superheater. There was a spacious cab. Below the running board the 2-8-2s were equipped with leading and trailing radial axles (the leading axle was placed close to the leading coupled axle to make the most of the limited ability of the former to follow curved track). This proved to be one of the few shortcomings of the design as the locomotives were punishing to the track. They also suffered rapid tyre wear. This was the result of their long fixed wheelbase and led to their permitted line speed being reduced from 25 to 20 mph for some years until curves could be eased. The Hd locomotives hauled the heavy trains across the Namib desert until the First World War reached

Above: *Freight traffic growth led to the introduction of the powerful Henschel Class Hd 2-8-2 tender locomotives in 1912. They were the last narrow gauge engines to cross the Namib desert to the coast, this approximately 100 mile portion of the railway being re-gauged to Cape Gauge after the 1915 invasion of the territory by South African armed forces.*
(Leith Paxton Collection)

Left: *This close-up of the valve gear of preserved Hd locomotive No.41 at Otjiwarongo shows the close proximity of the leading radial axle to the first coupled axle. Despite this the long fixed wheelbase of these engines proved damaging to the track.*
(David Payling)

South West Africa in 1915. They became the last narrow gauge locomotives to operate across the Namib desert from the port of Swakopmund. This was because the invading South African and British troops built a new Cape gauge (1067mm) line as they advanced from Walvis Bay to Swakopmund. They also rebuilt the now sabotaged narrow gauge Otavi Railway inland from the latter town to Usakos to the Cape gauge as the campaign progressed.

By the Summer of 1914 the German colony had reached the zenith of its prosperity. To enhance communications an order was placed with Henschel for two express passenger Pacific locomotives. They were designated as Class He, Nos.31 and 32. The pair were built at Kassel and passed to Woermann Lines for shipping from Germany to South West Africa. They never arrived! It is now known that they had been landed at Rio de Janeiro in Brazil to avoid the British blockade of the South West African coast. At Rio the two were eventually impounded by the Brazilian Government in 1917, following that country's declaration of war on Germany. The two

The Henschel works photograph of Otavi Pacific No.31, the Lord Lucan of the narrow gauge! Along with No.32 it was shipped by Woermann Lines from Hamburg in the Summer of 1914 and disappeared, never reaching South West Africa.
(NGRS Archive)

The two Otavi pacifics were in fact landed at Rio de Janeiro and were eventually placed in service with the Brazilian army railway regiment. This photo shows No.32 in its new working life, but still recognisable with its boiler top water purifier. (Eduard Coelho Collection)

locomotives then spent their working life with the railway regiment of the Brazilian army. It is a great pity that they never had the chance to show what a 600mm gauge pacific could do on the long straight runs on the Otavi!

After the war, the South African government was mandated by the League of Nations to administer the former German colony. Following this, in 1921, the Otavi Railway and the rest of the country's railway system was absorbed into the South African Railways (SAR). Meanwhile the peace had produced an upsurge in the demand for metals. To meet this extra traffic, a further batch of six Hd locomotives (now, however, classified by SAR as Class NG5) was delivered from Henschel in 1921 (Nos.71 - 76). The nine 2-8-2 NG5s now ran the mineral traffic on the newly shortened journey of some 256 miles northwards between Usakos and Tsumeb and its mines.

~ 3. The 2-8-2 Tender Mixed Traffic Engines, Class NG15 ~

Within South Africa, during the 1920s, the SAR CME's Department continued to develop its Garratt-based narrow gauge motive power strategy. South West Africa, however, was seen as a rather remote territory and the authorities at Windhoek and the workshops at Usakos enjoyed considerable autonomy. Nonetheless, it appears that one or more NG/G13s were sent to Usakos on trial for an extended period. They were possibly No.49 and/or No.50, bought as a supplement to the first NG/G13 order placed with Hanomag in 1927. No photographs have come to light as yet to confirm their work in the territory. Interestingly, however, evidence that this did indeed happen can be found in the annually produced SAR Private Working Time Books (working time tables). These contained weight tables for Garratt locomotives of NG/G13 power for trains between Usakos and Tsumeb. The NG/G13 entry appeared in each annual PWTB from 1929 to 1933, but was omitted from future editions. It perhaps suggests that the SAR management nearly succeeded in imposing their narrow gauge Garratt motive power policy on the territory.

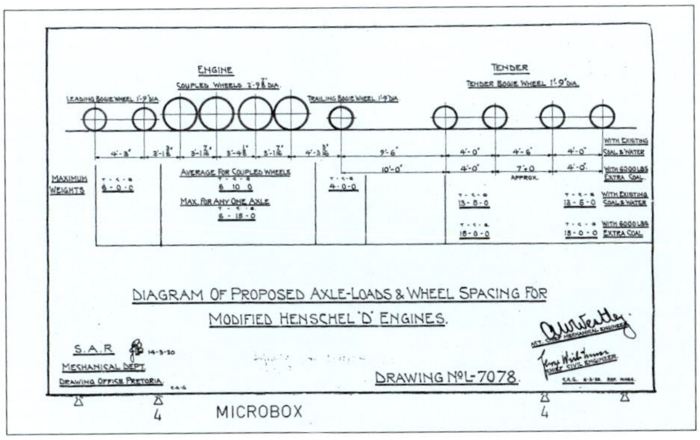

Left: *Early SAR documents (1930) show that a 4-8-2 tender locomotive design was considered for the NG15 before the Krauss-Helmholz bogie design was adopted for the 2-8-2 locomotive of 1931.* (David Payling Collection)

Below: *The works photograph of the pioneer NG15 locomotive No.17, 1931, shows several detail differences from later engines, the boiler top sand box being a prominent difference.* (Transnet Heritage Library)

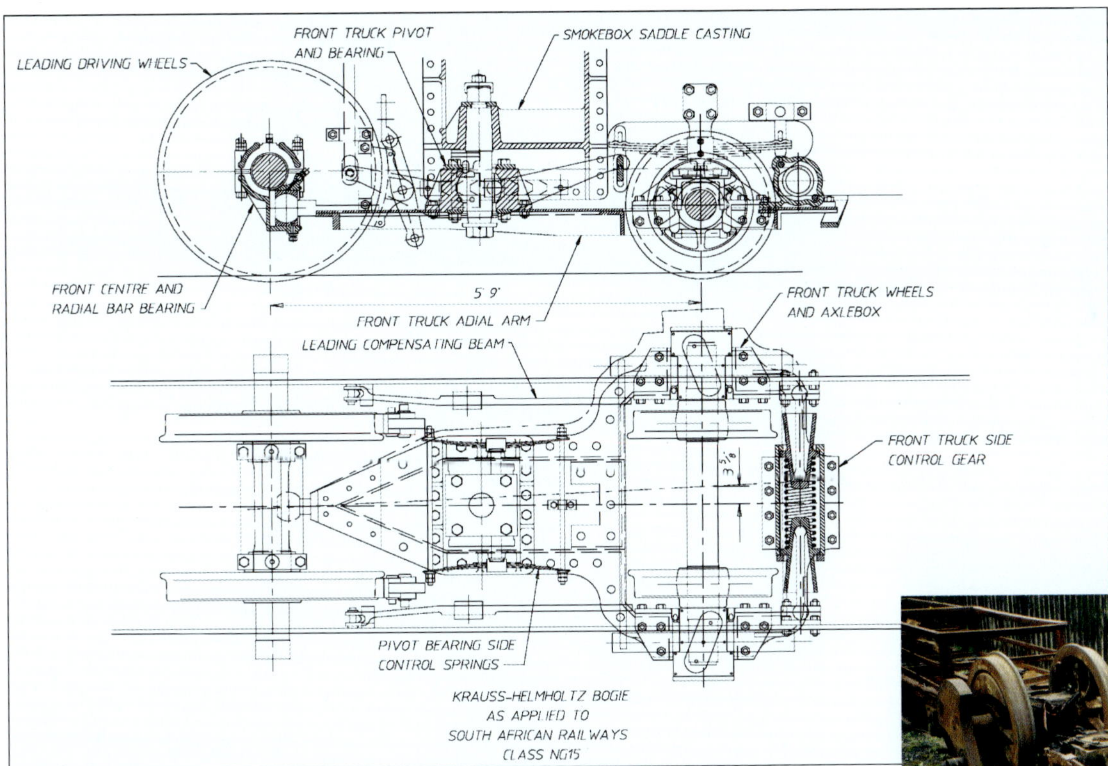

Above: *The Krauss-Helmholz bogie of the NG15s links the movement of the leading carrying axle and the first coupled axle, allowing the locomotive remarkable flexibility in negotiating sharply curved track.* (Leith Paxton)

Right: *A member of the Welsh Highland Heritage Railway imported No.120 in the early 1990s and were quick to strip down the engine for restoration. In 2001 this allowed the detail of the Krauss-Helmholz bogie to be seen.* (David Payling)

The works photograph of Anglo-Franco-Belge NG15 No.120 of 1950 shows the many detail differences from the 1931 batch of engines from Henschel. (Transnet Heritage Library)

In fact, however, the Usakos authorities had eventually won the argument for a continuation of their preference for powerful long range tender engines. In 1931 this resulted in the delivery by Henschel to Walvis Bay of the three pioneer NG15s, Nos.17 - 19. A further three arrived from Henschel in 1939 (Nos.117 - 119), although with small differences in specification. The differences included the repositioning of boiler water feed from the boiler sides to the boiler top, in front of the dome, and the transfer of the sand box and the turbo-electricity generator from the boiler top to the footplate. The American Pyle lighting equipment gave way to Stone's Tonum headlights. The shrill whistle supplied with the 1931 engines gave way to a SAR chime whistle.

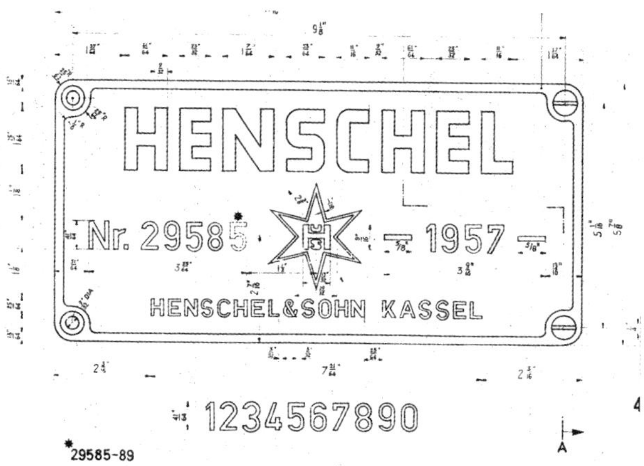

The NG15 design was very much based on the earlier NG5s, although with changes to overcome some of the limitations of the earlier engines. Documents of the period show that SAR management had considered various options, one being for a 4-8-2 tender engine, for which a weights diagram was prepared (see illustration on page 91). No real change was required to the free steaming boiler and firebox of the NG5 design, although the stove pipe chimneys gave way to a well proportioned flared, lipped chimney. The superheater became a three row fifteen element layout, allowing an update to the small tube layout.

The major changes, however, were to the chassis design. The leading and trailing radial axles were discarded in favour of pony trucks, the one beneath the firebox becoming a conventional, compensated Bissell truck. The key change however was the new design for the leading axle. In the new engines the leading axle was articulated to the front coupled axle in a Krauss-Helmholz bogie and this was the secret of the new design's success in coping with sharp track curvature. The leading coupled axle was able to move laterally through the axlebox horns by $^{31}/_{32}$ in, the eyes of the leading coupling rods allowing a corresponding lateral movement by the crank pins. This gave the locomotive a fixed wheelbase which effectively included only the rear three coupled axles. In fact it was now comparable in length to the fixed wheelbase of a NG/G16. The NG15s proved to be able freely to negotiate all of the SAR lines where they were eventually stationed. It could perhaps be said that the Kalaharis in North Wales represent yet another type of articulated steam locomotive!

The cab side of No.147 records the Tsumeb ownership of the locomotive during its service in Namibia. (Robin Lake)

As an additional refinement for long distance work the NG15 was equipped with an even larger tender than the NG5s. The water capacity remained 2860 gallons whilst 5½ tons of coal could also be carried. Rocking grates were provided and lights in the cab. A canvas sheet was rolled into the rear of the cab roof to provide cover from sun or rain, as required. Sanding was by gravity from sand boxes set into the footplate, although the first three engines carried a boiler top sand box for a short period after their delivery. Sight feed lubrication was provided and became standard for the whole class. It may have been felt that the massive slab sided tenders, with water pockets at the sides carried down almost to axlebox level, detracted somewhat from the overall appearance of the engines. If so, this might explain why, on some tenders, the outer upper sheeting was cut away by the Usakos workshops to give a swept-up line to the tender top. After the 1961 transfer of the engines to Port Elizabeth, the workshops at Uitenhage did not continue this practice, but allowed those already converted to remain in this condition.

After the Second World War two further batches were ordered. They were built by Société Anglo-Franco-Belge, Nos.120 - 124 being delivered in 1951 and Nos.132 - 136 in 1953. A final batch of five locomotives was supplied by Henschel in 1957 (TC1 - TC5, later becoming Nos.144 - 148), bringing the class total to twenty-one. Curiously, while all of the first sixteen locos carried standard SAR cab-side number plates bearing the NG prefix (e.g, NG134), the re-numbered Tsumeb engines had no prefix, being numbered 144-148.

The post-war engines carried fireboxes fitted with cross stays in the water space. These boilers can be recognised by a slanting row of six domed caps below the hand rail on the firebox side which gave clearance for the large nutted boss at the end of each stay. Boiler swaps during major workshop repairs have meant that the two types of boiler were fitted interchangeably to the twenty-one engines. At some point in the 1960s it was decided to convert the lubrication of the motion from oil to grease and this was extended to the whole fleet. Some of the engines also acquired sloping stays to brace the cab front to the running board. Unlike the post-war NG/G16s all of the Kalaharis were equipped with sight feed lubrication.

During the career of these engines in Southern Africa, management and footplate crews alike were swift to recognise the eager power and remarkable turn of speed of the NG15 locomotive. No major design weaknesses or defects emerged during their approximately 70 years of service. Charlie Lewis was SAR's Regional Civil Engineer in the Eastern Cape during the 1970s and 1980s. He experienced the work of the NG15s during his management of the rebuilding of the Avontuur Railway for the heavier axle load of Class 91 diesel locomotives. Later, as General Manager of the Alfred County Railway, his high regard for their work resulted in the ACR obtaining two NG15s for service in Natal. One of them was No.146, whose work won high praise from Phil Girdlestone, the ACR's Chief Mechanical Engineer. After his experience of the work of this engine on the Port Shepstone to Harding line, he stated that he would have preferred his second producer gas conversion to be a NG15, rather than a Garratt (No.155)! The NG15s have also won praise from users in Perth, Australia. Two of them had been bought from South Africa and can be seen at work on Perth's Bennett Brook Railway. The recently retired manager of the line, Mr Ross Parker, thought them to be the best designed locomotive for public 24 inch narrow gauge lines. These views give an encouraging prospect for their work in Snowdonia.

The works photograph of Henschel NG15 No.TC4, the penultimate locomotive of the class to be built.
(Leith Paxton Collection)

- XI -
The NG15s in Southern Africa

~ 1. South West Africa (Namibia) (1931 - 1960) ~

By the end of 1957, five batches of NG15s, a total of twenty-one locomotives, had been built for service on the Otavi Railway in South West Africa (SWA) –renamed Namibia since independence in 1990. The first batch of three engines, delivered in 1931, had sufficed, along with the nine NG5s, to cope with traffic on the line until 1939. Three more NG15s were added at this point although war-time soon brought a slowing of mining activity at Tsumeb. After the Second World War ownership of the mines by the Otavi Mining Company was replaced by the new Tsumeb Mining Corporation. The output of the mines now began to increase sharply. This produced the need to supplement the fleet by a further ten engines. Two new batches were therefore purchased, being delivered in 1951 and 1953. This time the builder was Société Anglo-Franco-Belge of La Croyère in Belgium, rather than Henschel of Germany. As the 1950s passed the mines required ever more railway capacity and negotiations began with SAR to increase the motive power available. At this time the railway authorities were unable to budget for additional locomotives rapidly enough to satisfy the mining corporation and an alternative arrangement was agreed. The Tsumeb Corporation would order five new engines from Henschel and they would be the property of the Corporation, although operated as part of the SAR fleet. When the Otavi Railway was converted to Cape gauge and dieselised, SAR guaranteed that they would then purchase the five engines for use on narrow gauge lines in South Africa.

Photographs of the NG15s in service in South West Africa are scarce. This classic image shows a predominantly passenger service forging through scrubby land behind No.118 at some time in the 1950s. (SAR/David Payling Collection)

Until the end of narrow gauge services in November 1960 the NG15s were all based at Usakos, the location of SWA's narrow gauge workshops. They were operated and maintained as a fleet although few details of this period of their career have been discovered so far. They had met every requirement of the operating department, hauling both heavy mixed and freight trains throughout the Otavi Railway system. This came to an end on 27th November 1960 with the completion of the conversion of the line to the Cape gauge.

Above: *Although the narrow gauge in SWA was rapidly approaching its end in the late 1950s, a further five NG15s were ordered from Henschel. Here, one of the five is seen in charge of a freight train, probably of agricultural produce. Note the cab-side Tsumeb corporation ownership plates.*
(SAR/David Payling Collection)

Left: *The last narrow gauge train reaches Otavi for a festive welcome. The date was Sunday 27th November 1960 and the two engines on the train were NG15s Nos.19 and 117. The headboard can still be seen today, preserved in Windhoek's TransNamib museum.*
(Walter Rusch Collection)

~ 2. Port Elizabeth (1961 - 1973) ~

The twenty-one NG15 locomotives arrived at Port Elizabeth on Cape gauge wagons early in 1961. The Uitenhage breakdown crane was employed to unload them onto the dockside's narrow gauge rails, where they were then hauled to the running shed at Humewood Road. They were re-commissioned and gradually introduced into service on the Avontuur Railway during 1961. The five 1957 Tsumeb engines were put into service later, in 1962; the Tsumeb plates on the cab sides having been replaced by SAR plates. As a class the engines now began to receive their workshop repairs at Uitenhage just to the north of Port Elizabeth. Transfers to and from Humewood Road running shed and the workshops were made on special Cape gauge wagons. These ancient vehicles had been equipped with rails welded to their decks and with removable bridging rail sections to allow rolling stock to be moved between wagons. A loading dock at the running shed allowed locomotives to be pushed directly onto the Cape gauge wagons without the use of a crane. At Uitenhage, workshop practice was geared to keeping as much of the fleet as possible in service at all times. There appears to have been just one spare boiler (supplied in 1951 by Anglo-Franco-Belge) for the NG15s. When a locomotive arrived at the workshops for heavy repair it would first of all have its boiler removed for attention. The chassis and running gear were relatively rapidly repaired compared with a boiler. The practice was therefore to fit a repaired boiler from the pool to the overhauled locomotive chassis. As a result it was unusual for a locomotive to leave the works after repair with the same boiler with which it had arrived.

The running shed at Humewood Road in Port Elizabeth was well equipped, even having a wheel drop available, in addition to the normal facilities for the maintenance fitters and boilermakers. Each locomotive had its own Repair Book. These were kept in the locomotive foreman's office and allowed the driver each day to record problems on his locomotive that would require attention from the depot fitters. There were also separately maintained boiler records for each locomotive.

The NG15s were an immediate success at Port Elizabeth, showing none of the drawbacks which had caused the pre-war trial of a NG5 (Hd) to be terminated when the long fixed wheelbase of the engine became jammed on curved track. The crews affectionately knew them as Kalaharis, although this was a misnomer. In South West Africa the locomotives had worked many hundreds of miles away from the Kalahari desert which lay to the South and East of the country. Indeed, they did not even work across the Namib desert, this part of the original Otavi Railway having been converted to the Cape gauge during 1915, some sixteen years before the appearance of the NG15s.

Above: *The NG15s travelled to Port Elizabeth from Usakos on Cape gauge wagons and were unloaded by the Uitenhage workshop's heavy rail mounted crane in the docks area.* (Leith Paxton)

Below: *During the 1960s the fleet of twenty-one NG15s were converted from oil lubrication of their motion to grease lubrication. The right hand side coupling rod bearings of No.135 are receiving attention from the driver's grease gun.* (Wally Greig)

At Port Elizabeth their arrival resulted in the withdrawal of the older locomotives including the Baldwin pacifics of Class NG10 (a closely similar Baldwin pacific, from the Pretoria Portland Cement line at Port Elizabeth, can be seen in preservation today in South Wales, running on the Brecon Mountain Railway). Also the work of the NG/G13 and NG/G16 Garratts became limited to the limestone traffic whose timetable required up to five Garratts working between Loerie and Chelsea Junction. The Garratts also worked trains in the more remote part of the line between Assegaaibos and Avontuur in the Langkloof. For the twelve years from 1961 to 1973 the NG15s were the dominant motive power for the main line between Assegaaibos and Port Elizabeth.

Left: *The NG15s and the NG/G13 Garratts shared the arduous work on a key freight flow of the Avontuur line, the limestone trains between Loerie and Chelsea Junction. In August 1962 one of the NG15s has been cut into the train after the ninth wagon, with five wagons and the guard's van trailing. In this scene they are climbing the twelve miles of the 1 in 40 bank from Loerie to Summit. They are probably travelling slowly enough for a fit engineman to jump down and run alongside the train for a while! In the loops at Summit the NG15 will be released to return down the bank light engine to await its next duty.* (Charlie Lewis)

The second of the three principal freight streams on the Avontuur line was deciduous fruit from the Langkloof. Whilst the limestone traffic ran year round the fruit was strictly seasonal. Here, Nos.134 and an unidentified NG15 depart Loerie for the docks at Port Elizabeth in April 1973. (Charlie Lewis)

The third principal freight was also seasonal and traffic began just as the deciduous fruit season came to an end, fortunately. Nos.136 and 146 head a train of empty box cars through Hankey, bound for the citrus fruit packing factory at Patensie in July 1985. (Charlie Lewis)

As well as the limestone, the Avontuur had a second year-round traffic. With just 17 miles left before reaching Avontuur, No.134 heads a short mixed train past Gaviota in June 1977. Even though passenger trains had ceased in the 1940s, it was still possible to travel in a passenger/guard's van on most trains. (Charlie Lewis)

~ 3. *Port Elizabeth (1973 - 1985)* ~

In 1973 the arrival of the Class 91 diesel electrics at Port Elizabeth provided the next milestone in the career of the NG15s. The entry into service of these twenty new General Electric diesels was the signal for the Garratts at Port Elizabeth to be retired from service whilst the NG15s now assumed a relatively minor role. Their remaining duties included the working of the Patensie branch with its citrus fruit traffic. They also powered a mixed passenger train service on this 17½ miles branch. Retention of the NG15s for this work was a consequence of the branch not having yet been upgraded with heavier rail (60lb per yard) to allow diesel running. For the same reason the NG15s also handled the traffic along

The first Great Train Race was held between Humewood Road and Loerie in August 1979. On this occasion the train was the winner and the victorious crew are seen here receiving the trophy. The train engine on the day was the immaculately turned out NG15 No.124, complete with ornamental smoke deflectors, headboard, highly polished brass headlight and oil lamps. (Bruce Brinkman)

In the early 1980s the Apple Express prepares to leave Humewood Road station in Port Elizabeth behind Kalahari No.124. Note the heavy headboard of solid brass (it took two to lift it!) and the small decorative smoke deflectors carried at this time. This became a progressively important duty for the NG15s as the 1980s advanced. (Bruce Brinkman)

the 77 miles of the main line beyond Assegaaibos in the Langkloof, including its heavy deciduous fruit traffic of apples, pears, peaches and apricots, etc. This gave sufficient work to keep the whole class busy in traffic. Although this traffic grew year by year the mileage run by the NG15s contracted each year as the Class 91s were enabled by the new track to penetrate ever further towards Avontuur. This remained the situation until 1985 when the fruit growers in the Langkloof transferred their traffic from rail to road. Henceforth the fruit was trucked westwards to Cape Town for shipping instead of eastwards to Port Elizabeth. This calamitous loss of custom had coincided with completion of upgrading the line to Avontuur with new, heavier rail to support the 11 ton axle load of the Class 91s. After 1986 the now diesel hauled traffic between Avontuur and Assegaaibos dwindled away until regular services ceased running in 1991.

~ 4. *Port Elizabeth (1986 - 2011)* ~

With the loss of the fruit traffic from the Langkloof and the completion of rebuilding the main line for diesel traction, by 1985 there was little work left for the NG15s. There was a plan to run a steam-hauled museum service between Loerie and Patensie on the still lightly laid track on the branch. The planned upgrading of the 17½ miles branch from Gamtoos Junction with heavier rail had been abandoned when the deciduous fruit service on the neighbouring line through the Langkloof collapsed in 1985. This new service was to be in conjunction with a planned narrow gauge museum at Humewood Road station. In the event the museum project was abandoned. Meanwhile, however, steam repairs at Uitenhage had ceased in 1985 and in July 1990 the daily steam service had to be abandoned as a result of steam maintenance difficulties at the running shed. This left only the haulage of the Apple Express which had been initiated in May 1965 under the auspices of SAR. It was a tourist steam service powered generally by the NG15s. The trains started from Humewood Road station in Port Elizabeth and ran to various destinations including Thornhill and Loerie. Favourite locomotives for this service were red-liveried No.122 which carried the name *Star King* on small smoke deflectors. Green liveried No.124 likewise became *Granny Smith*. Trains made a single return trip per day at weekends and on certain weekdays, especially during Port Elizabeth's holiday season of December and January.

During the early 1990s South African Transport Services gave notice that the Apple Express would cease to run. The Alfred County Railway in Natal became involved briefly, maintaining continuity of the service. However, the longer term responsibility for promoting, organising and crewing the Apple Express trains was then taken up by the newly established Apple Express Society of local volunteers. The Society continued in this role, although under progressively restrictive regulatory and financial arrangements, until December 2010. Locomotive repairs and maintenance had became an increasingly difficult issue for the Society and the last two NG15s in service, green liveried No.124 and black No.145, were taken out of service for overhaul during 1999. They were replaced in service by NG/G16 No.131. This engine had been one of the last in South Africa to receive a workshop overhaul. It had worked for many years in Natal and had been transferred, freshly overhauled, to Port Elizabeth as part of the abortive museum scheme. Garratt No.131 now shouldered the Apple Express steam-hauled services exclusively. One of its last duties was its involvement in a 2005 rail tour, the Avontuur Adventurer. This made a rare (and possibly one of the last) visit to Avontuur, some 177 miles distant from Port Elizabeth, in September 2005. Jointly promoted by the Apple Express and the Sandstone Heritage Trust, the tour also featured the doyen of the NG15 class, No.17, which had been restored recently by the Sandstone organisation. Both engines ran immaculately although, by this time,

Left: *Passengers on the Avontuur Adventurer of September 2005 spent the first night of the tour at Patensie, at the end of the branch from Gamtoos Junction 17½ miles away. Here, Sandstone's No.17 makes a thunderous start to the second day as it leaves Patensie bound for Assegaaibos and the Langkloof.* (David Payling)

Below: *The third day of the Avontuur Adventurer saw the train deep in the Langkloof valley. No.17 passes orchards in the foreground yet to come into leaf, whilst the Goukama mountains to the North form the background.* (Alan Buttrum)

No.131 was well overdue for mechanical and boiler overhaul. The honour of hauling the Avontuur Adventurer into both Patensie and onwards to Avontuur fell to No.17. The tour proved to be a truly memorable occasion which now may have become impossible to repeat.

Garratt No.131 was eventually withdrawn for firebox repairs later in 2005. Although some years of Class 91 diesel haulage of the Apple Express now followed, it became possible to restore steam haulage in November 2008. The locomotive concerned was 1939-built NG15 No.119. Although laid aside for overhaul many years ago this locomotive had been restored to working order through the unstinting efforts of the Society. Its supporters in local government had also provided backing with modest State funding. Sadly, this initiative came to an end on 29th December 2010 when No.119 hauled the final Apple Express train from Humewood Road to Loerie and return. National and local government support had been abruptly withdrawn earlier during the year. In 2012 it remains to be seen whether the Apple Express volunteers can revive this beacon of hope for narrow gauge preservation and tourist operation in South Africa.

One of the official initiatives of the 1980s and early 1990s had been to offer surplus NG15 locomotives and other rolling stock for sale. Eventually a number of NG15s were sold out of service (Appendix 4) although, so far, only four have been returned to service. These include Nos.118 and 123 on the Bennett Brook Railway in Perth, Australia, and No.18 at a private location in Houston, Texas. More recently No.17, the class pioneer of 1931, has been restored to service at the Sandstone Heritage Railway in the Eastern Free State. Nos.133 and 134 have been at Dinas since April 1998, whilst No.135 is owned by the Exmoor Steam Railway and Nos.201, 121 and 146 are part of the late Peter Rampton's collection.

Right: *29th December 2010 saw the last run by the Apple Express from Port Elizabeth to Loerie and return. No.119 is seen here with the train on the journey to Loerie, crossing the van Stadens bridge, famously the highest 24 in. gauge railway bridge in the world.* (Alan Buttrum)

Inset: *Whilst No.119 was busy with the final Apple Express train of 2010, No.124 was under overhaul and nearing completion inside the Humewood Road diesel depot, a quarter of a mile beyond the Humewood Road steam depot and passenger station.* (Alan Buttrum)

~ 5. No. 120 in Southern Africa ~

The first of the post-war built NG15s was Anglo-Franco-Belge No.120. It arrived at Walvis Bay harbour for onward transport to Usakos on Cape gauge wagons on 14th March 1951. It was the first engine of the five in this batch and, after commissioning, was put to work on the Otavi Railway in South West Africa. It worked there with its sisters for the next nine years, hauling mineral and mixed trains between the trans-shipment facilities at Usakos and the mines at Tsumeb and the branch to Grootfontein. Together with the twenty other NG15s, the locomotive was duly transferred to Port Elizabeth in 1961 after the gauge conversion of the Otavi Railway.

At Port Elizabeth, in 1962, the camera of Charlie Lewis captured its return from an early visit to the Uitenhage workshops, piggy back on an ancient Cape gauge flat wagon. Little is known of its work on the Avontuur line over the next 25 years. Fortunately, however, although the repair books for this engine have not been traced, it has been possible to obtain photocopies of its boiler records from a private collection in Port Elizabeth. These records show that in November 1976 No.120 returned from its final SAR workshop repairs.

With the new fleet of diesels already operating much of the traffic over the first 100 miles of the railway, most of the work of No.120

Below: *No.120 was given workshop attention before entering service at Port Elizabeth. It is seen here in April 1962 awaiting unloading at Humewood Road after its journey from the workshops at Uitenhage.* (Charlie Lewis)

Bottom: *One of the main traffics on the Avontuur line was deciduous fruit from the Langkloof. The photograph shows a loaded train led by No.120 gingerly descending the difficult section of line near Heights in April 1982. By this date many of the fruit wagons had been increased in height to facilitate palletised loading.* (Dick Manton)

was now in the more remote part of the Langkloof beyond Assegaaibos along the 77 miles to Avontuur, and also on the Patensie branch. The work in the Langkloof included powering the works trains that were upgrading the track and clearances for the new diesels. The busiest time of the year was the peak fruit season when the NG15s brought loaded trains from the Langkloof down to the ships at Port Elizabeth. On the Patensie Branch there was similar seasonal work bringing the citrus fruit for export via Port Elizabeth docks. The final year of No.120's hydraulic certificate was 1985 and thereafter the engine was laid aside, stored at Humewood Road running shed.

On 7 October 1994 No. 120 was imported to the UK by Peter Thomasson, member of the Welsh Highland Light Railway (1964) Ltd, now Welsh Highland Railway Ltd trading as Welsh Highland Heritage Railway. It was moved to the company's Gerlert's Farm depot and dismantled for restoration. Following the owner's death in 2001 it was donated to the company, which sold it in 2009.

~ 6. No. 133 in Southern Africa ~

The second batch of post-war NG15s arrived in 1953. No.133 was delivered new from Anglo-Franco-Belge at La Croyère in Belgium on 30th September of that year. It was landed at Walvis Bay in South West Africa and transferred to the narrow gauge workshops at Usakos some 93½ miles inland from Swakopmund. Here it joined the earlier NG15s and their predecessors, the NG5s, working the long narrow gauge line from Usakos to the copper mines at Tsumeb, together with the branches to Outjo and Grootfontein.

Having been displaced from its work in remote Namibia, No.133 arrived at Port Elizabeth in the early months of 1961. The next fifteen years were spent working on the Avontuur line. By a happy chance F&WHR director, Mike Hart, was recently

Top Right: *No.120 is seen at Gelert's Farm in Porthmadog in October 1994 after its arrival from Port Elizabeth. The locomotive was later stripped down to its components for overhaul.* (David Allan)

Right: *No photographs of No.133 at work in SWA have so far come to light and this scene on 6th October 1962 is one of the earliest at Port Elizabeth, showing the engine ready for duty at Humewood Road steam running shed.* (Leith Paxton)

Above: *By 1974 No.133 was looking work-stained as it stood in Humewood Road running shed on 10th September.* (Tony Leeson)

Left: *Deep in the Langkloof, No.133 passes Bruinklip with a mixed train for Avontuur in July 1978. The locomotive, together with several other NG15s, retains the tender modifications it had received at Usakos during the 1950s.* (Charlie Lewis)

able to acquire the Repair Books for both No.133 and No.134. They have been copied and the originals placed in the Drawing Office at Boston Lodge. They are historic documents of quite considerable interest in that they form a record of the mishaps, frequent or rare, which the engines were prone to suffer. Separately, the original boiler certificates from 1961 to the late 1980s have also been obtained for both Nos.133 and 134.

The Repair Book for No.133 runs from 19th November 1982 to the date the engine was taken out of service, 13th November 1986. The earliest record in its boiler certificate file dates from 1972 when the locomotive was admitted to Uitenhage for a Heavy General repair. At this overhaul its boiler, No.10613 (first carried by newly built No.135, Anglo-Franco-Belge, 1953), was replaced by boiler No. 10611 (built for No.133, Anglo-Franco-Belge, 1953). The locomotive then ran uneventfully (according to the boiler records)

Left: *During the 1980 apple season up to fourteen NG15s were outstationed at Assegaaibos to operate the fruit trains at the top end of the line. No.133 is seen heading a train of empty fruit wagons towards Louterwater. Additional engine crews were drafted in from Cape gauge work at Port Elizabeth for the fruit season and No.133 had a regular crew who, on their own initiative, kept their loco cleaned and polished to perfection. By the 1981 season heavier rail had reached Louterwater allowing diesels to be used which considerably reduced the number of steam locos required.* (Dick Manton)

Left: *No.133 heads a loaded train of fruit cars through Joubertina, passing the plinthed NG/G13 locomotive, No.80. By 1980 this NG15 had been coupled to an unmodified flat sided tender.* (Dick Manton)

Below: *No.133 hurries a train of fruit through the Langkloof. As the track gang advanced towards Avontuur, preparing the line for diesel locomotives, the steam hauled trains had an ever shorter run before handing over to diesel haulage for the rest of the journey to Port Elizabeth.* (Dick Manton)

until June 1979 when it entered Uitenhage for what was to be its last General Repair. According to the locomotive Repair Book the Humewood Road Mechanical Foreman had requested that repairs should include alignment of the engine frames and tender bogie frames, plus renewal of the front and rear pony truck kingpin bushes. Special repairs were also to include the renewal of the internal steam

Left: *Two wagons of ballast are being shunted at Heights in April 1980. These Class Y wagons were built for the Avontuur line improvement in the 1970s. Thereafter they did little work. The WHR was fortunate to acquire two. Sadly the majority have now been scrapped, the difficulty of exporting narrow gauge items having been too difficult to overcome.*
(Dick Manton)

pipe and branch steam pipes, plus the sand boxes and the intermediate drag box bushes. The boiler fitted was the newly repaired No.8684 (first carried by No.17, Henschel, 1931). Repairs to this boiler had included the patching of the foundation corners of the inner firebox back plate and replacement of half of the side plates. The outer firebox and boiler barrel were de-scaled. Some 334 rigid steel stays were replaced and the palm stays were overhauled. The tubes and superheater flues were all replaced, as were the smokebox wrapper and liner and the spark arrestor.

After boiler certification tests on 16th July 1979 the locomotive was released to traffic and was soon back at work hauling freights in the Langkloof between Assegaaibos and Avontuur. The next few years were punctuated by 15-monthly mechanical examinations and annual re-certification of the boiler. The file for No.133 ends with the re-certification of its boiler for twelve months from 23rd July 1986, although the inspector had recorded minor wastage of the lower tubes in the smokebox. The final entry in the Driver's Repair Book is dated 13th November 1986 when attention to the pony truck was requested and provided. After this the records simply cease and provide no clue as to why No.133 was taken out of traffic. The boiler still had nearly three years of its hydraulic test life remaining before repair was due and the repair books showed no major problems looming. It seems likely that the real issue was that there was simply no longer enough work to keep all the NG15s busy. The whole of the Langkloof traffic had been dieselised by 1985. The Apple Express and the operation of the nineteen mile Patensie Branch with its seasonal fruit traffic and daily mixed trains would require few locomotives. Perhaps No.133 was not just lucky enough to remain on the active list?

~ 7. No. 134 in Southern Africa ~

The third member of the 1953 batch of Anglo-Franco-Belge NG15s was No.134, arriving at Walvis Bay harbour on 5th December 1953. It was duly transferred to Usakos on Cape gauge wagons for commissioning, before entering traffic. Seven years later, together with its twenty sister locomotives, it was displaced from this work by the gauge broadening of the Otavi Railway, completed in November 1960.

At Port Elizabeth, the existing Repair Book for No.134 covers the period from 14th April 1988 to 6th November 1990, the last entry recording that the engine was "stabled" on 15th October of that year. The recent discovery of the boiler certificates for No.134 is particularly fortunate since they confirm the identity of the boiler currently carried on this engine. Normally SAR locomotives carried a boiler data plate attached to the left hand side of the smokebox. This recorded the identity of the boiler and was stamped with the date of its last nine year hydraulic test and the dates of subsequent annual testing. On the WHR the boiler data plates are present on four of the NG/G16 Garratts (Nos.87, 138, 140 and 143) and on two of the NG15s: No.120, lately at Gelert's Farm, and No.133 at Dinas. However, the data plate for the boiler of No.134 was missing when the locomotive arrived at Dinas from the Pickering Steam Museum. These documents have made it possible to establish the identity of No.134's boiler, together with its maintenance history, making it more readily certifiable for the future.

After the arrival of No.134 at Port Elizabeth in 1961 the first surviving boiler certificate had been issued after its workshop general repair in 1972. It shows that the boiler carried up to that year was No.8685 (built for No.18, Henschel, 1931). After

No photographs of No.134 at work on the Otavi Railway have so far come to light. One of the earliest views of the engine at Port Elizabeth shows it at Humewood Road running shed, still with its modified tender and Stone's Tonum headlight. (Charlie Lewis)

Top left: *Much of the work of No.134 in its early days at Port Elizabeth was on the main line to the Langkloof. It is seen here in June 1962 at the old servicing depot at Assegaaibos.* (Charlie Lewis)

Top right: *Near Assegaaibos, No.134 is in charge of a mixed freight on the way to Avontuur.* (Charlie Lewis)

Left: *This August 1962 photograph shows No.134 climbing the eight miles long 1 in 40 Loerie bank with a mixed train of fruit and passenger vehicles for Port Elizabeth.* (Charlie Lewis)

Below: *Ten years after its arrival at Port Elizabeth No.134 is seen at Humewood Road running shed on 29th October 1971. It ran for a brief period in the early 1970s "embellished" with a dartboard design on the smokebox whilst the Stone headlight has been exchanged for twin sealed beam headlights.* (Leith Paxton)

repair No.134 returned to traffic in August 1972 with boiler No.10612 (built for No.134, Anglo-Franco-Belge, 1953). After this the locomotive received annual inspections at Humewood Road depot including renewal of side rod bushes together with other mechanical repairs. Intermediate repairs followed at Uitenhage in September 1975 and 1979, mainly involving repairs and maintenance of the running gear and chassis. The final Uitenhage Heavy General Repair and boiler exchange was completed on 29th September 1981, no unusual repairs or renewals being required to the chassis. The boiler allocated was No.7043 (built for No.144, Henschel, 1957). The boiler repairs had included patches to the steel inner firebox back plate foundation corners. The inner firebox side plates had been renewed, as had the front tube plate. Some 426 stays had been replaced together with forty rigid crown stays and three flexible crown stays. The palm stays had been overhauled and the gusset stays and cross stays examined. All of the boiler tubes and flue tubes were new. The fusible plug sockets had been re-tapped and fitted with new plugs. The inside surfaces of the barrel had been de-scaled.

After its return to traffic boiler certificates were issued annually for No.134 without any work being required on the boiler until 1988 when wastage was noted in the firebox tube plate. It was sufficiently minor to need no more than being kept under observation. This period in the life of No.134 included the end of its regular work between Assegaaibos and Avontuur in the Langkloof where Class 91 diesel electrics had taken over in 1984. Thereafter No.134's duties included Apple Express haulage from Humewood Road to Thornhill or to Loerie, plus regular work on the Patensie Branch.

Above: *In 1971 No.134 was captured leading another NG15 in the descent of Loerie bank with a train mainly consisting of fruit empties for the Langkloof. In South Africa it was the custom to run the NG15s chimney first, turntables or triangles being installed at strategic points.* (Leith Paxton)

Inset: *No.134 comes down the hill into Loerie, double heading with a class-mate on a train of fruit empties for the West. The photographer is standing in the bunker of one of Loerie's NG/G13s waiting for the single line with a loaded train of limestone for Chelsea Junction and the Port Elizabeth cement factory.* (Leith Paxton)

Left: *No.134 stands in Loerie station with a mixed freight train for the Langkloof in 1971. The dust covered line in the foreground carries the limestone traffic from the loading bunkers at the West end of the station towards Chelsea and the twelve miles private line to the cement factory.* (Leith Paxton)

Below left: *In this July 1980 view No.134 has reverted to standard black SAR livery and has acquired a standard tender. It is heading a mixed train for Avontuur through Bruinklip.* (Charlie Lewis)

Much citrus fruit traffic originated on this branch and there was also a daily mixed train service. Plans to upgrade the branch with 60 lb. per yard rail had been abandoned when the deciduous fruit traffic in the Langkloof had been lost to road hauliers, also in 1984. One consequence was the barring of the branch to the Class 91 diesels with their 11 tons axle load. Steam operation therefore continued for another five years on a "museum" basis, making a virtue out of necessity! The service ended only in July 1990 and, from this date, the Class 91s were approved to work to Patensie, although at a much reduced speed.

In September 1990, just three months after the cessation of the Patensie steam service, the boiler certificate of No.134 was renewed, but only for a period of twenty nine days, eventually ending on 28th October when its 9-yearly hydraulic certificate expired. After this a small amount of running shed work is recorded on the boiler summary sheet. This may explain why the boiler of No.134 showed evidence of repairs in progress at the time of its arrival in North Wales. For example there were blanking plates covering some of the boiler openings and both the cladding sheets and insulation had been removed. According to the record a final inspection of the boiler had been made on 2nd July 1991 and a further note made of the wastage of the firebox tube plate, plus the need for a complete re-tube. Rather than carry out these repairs a Stop Certificate was issued and the certificate marked with the recommendation that the locomotive be withdrawn from service.

- XII -
Returning No.134 to Traffic

~ Peter Randall, Leader of the WHRS No.134 Project ~

NG15 No. 133 at Dinas on 18 April 1998. (Peter Johnson)

For most people, 30th March 2006 was not a notable day. I was an exception! Arriving at 08:30 in Johannesburg for my first visit to South Africa, I was greeted at the airport by Niki and whisked away with three others to join the Cosmos event at Sandstone. This is a farm estate in the middle of the high veldt of the Free State at Ficksburg, about half way between Bethlehem and Bloemfontein. Here the Sandstone Heritage Trust has established a working museum of agricultural, military and railway artefacts, most of which are in full working order. There are traction engines, road rollers, a steam crane, a team of oxen, threshing machines, a couple of old buses, armoured cars, personnel carriers, and a working Sherman tank, to name but a few - but the "pièce de résistance" is the 30km long 2 foot gauge railway. This boasts over twenty working locos, from the smallest, a diminutive Decauville 0-4-0T, to the might of four NG/G13 and NG/G16s (all four operated together in tandem last year!), plus literally hundreds of wagons.

The Cosmos flower event itself has passed into folklore and here is not the place to recount the adventures of that week. However the journey there turned out to be my "road to Damascus". For years I had looked with fascination at the NG15s at Dinas and wondered what they might be capable of and now I was about to find out! On arrival at Hoekfontein, the centre of the estate, there, sitting in the platform, was No.17, the first-built of the NG15 class, in steam and raring to go. Its black bulk and low centre of gravity, sheer size and latent power were overwhelming. Love at first sight does not do justice to my emotions at the time. Over the next week I came to appreciate that this creature was not just elegant and massive (for 2 foot gauge). It was also an extremely capable machine which could match virtually anything that the NG/G16s could do over the extremely demanding circuit that is Sandstone. Thus began an adventure which still has no ending.

Two NG15s had been imported into the UK in January 1998: they were Nos.133 and 134. They had been intended for a railway scheme planned to run on the Yorkshire coast using the old NER track bed of the Whitby to Scarborough line through Robin Hood's Bay. The scheme had unfortunately run into difficulties and then been abandoned. Its rolling stock had been put up for sale and Mike Schumann funded the purchase of the NG15s for the Welsh Highland Railway. Hence the presence of the brooding bulk of No.133 which has dominated the Dinas station scene for the last 15 years.

Over the years the gigantic hulks of Nos.133 and 134 slowly rusted and faded in the yard at Dinas. Rumours began to grow about their unsuitability and performance limitations. Why else were they not being restored? But the truth was fairly simple. The F&WHR management had decided on a policy of standardisation using the NG/G16s and, while there were sufficient of these, there was no place for an NG15 in the restoration queue. Gossip however does not let fact get in the way of a good story and so the rumours developed to the point where they overtook fact. The suggestions were that the NG15s were unable to run tender first and primed badly when running down-hill chimney first. There were also issues that - while not being a problem in South Africa - were a considerable challenge in North Wales. The large open back to the cab is a godsend in the warm climate of the Republic. In the Principality

By the time No.133 arrived at Dinas it had been paired with a slab sided tender. It is seen here in the bay platform in 1999, cosmetically restored and awaiting attention. (David Payling)

Above: *NG15 No. 134 at Dinas on 7 June 1998, as it was received.* (Peter Johnson)

however it simply ensures that "Welsh Sunshine" (that all-pervasive drizzle that can permeate the highest quality waterproofs) gets everywhere. The tender design, with enough water to do a trip from Caernarfon to Porthmadog two and a half times, is quite adequate until you work out how much coal you need to burn to drag all of that water three times from sea level to the summit near Rhyd Ddu! Secondly, the coal, spread evenly over the top of the 30 foot tender, is difficult to get to without the local South African gentlemen who used to ride on the back and move it forward for the fireman's convenience. All in all, perhaps it was right that these giants should moulder in a latter day Dai Woodham's yard, awaiting the grim reaper's "Manchester Hammer" (a gas axe, or oxyacetylene cutter).

Back to 2006 and Sandstone. Over the week and a half that we were there, the rest of the team and I, all experienced WHR people, took turns at handling the NG15. We tackled curves, gradients and loads which we will never see on the WHR. The railway on the farm is an excellent test for any locomotive. It is new, there being no historic narrow gauge railway in the area, but it does serve a practical purpose. The line runs from the main farm centre to and from interchange sidings on the SAR main line where it is possible to exchange goods. The railway has been used on numerous occasions to assist with the harvest, shipping grain from the fields where it was harvested, back to the silos at the farm centre. To access the SAR at Vailima from the farm at Hoekfontain, a steep ridge has to be crossed. This results in a tortuous climb at grades of up to 1 in 30 with reverse curves at critical points. To create even more of a challenge, the climb is approached from a 90° curve with a level crossing at its centre – limiting the approach speed. In 2006 (the alignment has since been much improved) there was also no cant on the curve! The climb presented a real challenge for the locomotive and the crew. However, during the week, we all became convinced of the ability of the NG15 to master the task. Thus began the quest to bring one of these locomotives into operation on the WHR.

While there may appear (to the casual observer passing Dinas) to have been little progress over the ensuing years, there have in fact been several attempts to restore these engines. There can be no criticism of the teams attempting these restorations. For a project of this magnitude one needs the support of major bodies and substantial funding, as well as the "political" will to see the job done.

Initially, when the locos first arrived in Wales, they were put on display in the yard at Dinas. Since then this has been the sole lot for No.133, apart from a brief interlude in a starring role, when it went to Caernarfon in 2009 to stand in the town square (Y Maes), looking very dominant, to assist fund raising. Its sister, No.134, has almost been hidden from sight, being the subject of the restoration projects from an early date. No.134 had arrived shortly after No.133, looking rather more care-worn than its sister but, as is often the case, looks can be deceptive. Detailed surveys of the two locomotives identified No.134 as the one in better condition so it was No.134 that was selected for initial overhaul. The work was started on a "no budget" basis in 1999 pending the completion of Garratt K1, then the current focus of loco funding appeals by the Society. Nonetheless donations were received for items such as boiler tubes and washout plugs. Numerous spares had also been acquired from South Africa to replace missing items on both locos, such as injectors and vacuum ejectors. The volunteers worked for a couple

Left: *On its arrival at Dinas, No.134 was found to have been partially prepared for boiler overhaul, the cladding and lagging having been removed and blanking plates applied to some of the boiler outlets. In 1999 it is seen, together with its tender chassis, in the locomotive shed head shunt during the first phase of its restoration to work on the WHR.* (David Payling)

of years and did much of the dismantling of the locomotive. The tender body was removed. Both tenders were in poor condition and, given the need to rebuild them to suit WHR conditions, the old tender body of No.134 was dumped at the back of the South yard, resting on sleepers. This initial work did not reveal any unpleasant surprises; indeed, quite the opposite! It is thought that No.134 might have been overhauled soon before withdrawal in South Africa, as its mechanical condition and the general condition of the boiler were found to be excellent.

As with all loco projects, as soon as one mentions a redesign, supporters spring into life and produce a myriad of designs and liveries for the engine. At this point several schemes were under consideration, including one which suggested transforming it into a tank engine! The late Handel Kardas ("Young Isambard" of Railway World magazine, and a great supporter of the WHR) joined in and produced a design resembling the type of bogie tender seen with some Southern Railway Maunsell designs (e.g. the S15 class 4-6-0), with the addition of a removable

Above: *By November 2003 No.134 had reached the end of the first stage of its restoration, having received attention from volunteers including Team Wylfa. It is seen here, awaiting further restoration, in the bay sidings at Dinas.*
(Ben Fisher, WHR Project Website)

Above *On 5th October 2005 the chassis was moved into the Clip Shed to allow work to begin on its overhaul.* (Roger Benn)

cab back (similar to the FR's *Linda*). Tenders however are very expensive and therefore there was no possibility of progressing the idea at that stage.

By January 2001, the group was making progress. It is interesting to read a contemporary report: "Cylinder bores and pistons were found to be in excellent condition. The valve chests were re-bored; new valve heads (and possibly spindles) would be needed. The motion was ready; the valve gear was overhauled with new pins and bushes where necessary; brasses on the connecting and coupling rods were found to be in "good as new" condition. Work remained to be done on axleboxes and suspension. Although a detailed official inspection by the insurers was awaited, it was believed that the boiler would need little more work than a re-tube, plus new superheater flues and elements, and routine work such as internal cleaning and renewal of studs. New crinolines (the framework to which boiler cladding sheets are fixed) were made and new boiler cladding was also started (the loco had arrived without any). The footplate and lower cab were completed, with work started on the upper part of the cab (detachable on SAR 2' gauge locos, so as to be within the loading gauge when transported on 3'6" gauge wagons). The tender chassis was repaired together with one of its bogies, with work also done on the other. The other major work left is the tender superstructure and loco pipe runs".

The first setback was approaching, however. The WHR was expanding rapidly. By July 2000, the first trains were running to Waunfawr. As the railway progressed, the demand for space in the Dinas loco shed increased. The WHR needed two engines in steam by this time, and the luxury of a no-cost volunteer project occupying precious space in the running shed was not tenable. Momentum was also gathering around the return of K1. Its new boiler

Above: *With the boiler now separated from the chassis, by 15th August 2004, it had been returned to the end of the bay platform siding at Dinas to stand alongside No.133.* (Ben Fisher, WHR Project Website)

Below: *Once inside the Clip Shed work began to dismantle the chassis. It is seen here, jacked clear of the wheels and axles. The Krauss-Helmholz bogie and the leading coupled axle were the last to be released, January 2009.* (Laurence Armstrong)

Bottom: *With the frames lifted, the wheel sets could be moved away, eventually to find their way to Boston Lodge for re-profiling.* (John Ellis Williams)

had been ordered and was due for delivery in 2002, so it was not too surprising when No.134 had to be moved out of the loco shed. Thereafter work stopped for the first, but not the last, time.

Work restarted in Autumn 2003, once again on a "no cost" basis. The work was led by the "Team Wylfa" volunteers, a group of engineers working at the power station on Anglesey. The boiler was protected by closing its various openings, and a comprehensive catalogue was made of the parts - both those refurbished during the previous programme and those still needing attention. A container in the South Yard was equipped with shelves to store them securely.

With the small parts secure and the loco chassis outdoors (and with no space available in the workshops), attention was turned to the tender chassis. The chassis was duly moved into the Goods Shed in late November 2003. Some work had already been undertaken, but was far from complete. The bogies needed to be swapped (they were the wrong way round), and the wheel sets needed to be removed for re-profiling to correct the gauge. Whilst nominally the same gauge, the South African Railways in fact operated at 2 foot gauge (610mm), while the WHR uses the traditional FR gauge of 1 ft. 11½ in. (597mm). This does not usually need the wheels to be shifted on the axles, a re-profiling to the FR standard being sufficient. This, however, revealed a much bigger problem. The wheels were not the same size! While one pair was virtually brand new, two of the others were at scrap size and one was not too far behind with about a quarter of its life left. Wheels need to be of similar size both for smooth running and vehicle stability. Braking with an oversized wheel set will result in overheating and loose tyres – highly undesirable. Clearly a solution to this was needed, but it would be many years later that the issue was finally resolved.

In January 2004 the team started work on the

bogie frames. They were found be in a "well used condition" and were going to need a lot of work to return the critical parts, the bearings and horn guides, to correct tolerances. Meanwhile the frames were cleaned, scraped and sanded back to bare metal and had their first paint for probably thirty years. The bogies and tender frame were reassembled, so that it was mobile, but with considerable work left to do before it would be complete.

At a meeting with the General Manager in February 2004 it was agreed that limited Company funds would be made available. This was to ensure that jobs would be done just once rather than the practice of removal, cleaning and reassembly without replacement of worn components. Buoyed by this boost and the arrival of Spring, attention turned back to the locomotive; the boiler was lifted off the frames in early April. The lift came courtesy of the crane that had cleared the containers from the remaining Phase 3 construction sites. The job was less easy than it sounds. The footplating had to be removed first and then the boiler securing bolts. These were badly rusted and many had to be burned out. Eventually the boiler was released and placed in the yard where it has remained for the last seven years. The frames were shunted back briefly to their place in the sidings

The boiler is newer than the rest of the loco, having been built for one of the 1957 batch of NG15s originally built for the Tsumeb Corporation. South African boiler records show that it had received major attention to the firebox in 1981, ten years before the loco came out of service, with renewal of the rear tubeplate and the inner firebox wrapper sides (plus of course the associated stays). In contrast to the WHR's 1997 misfortunes with the NG/G16 boilers, No.134's boiler seems to be in good condition.

On 6th April 2004 the tender bogie frames were swapped around so that they are now in their correct original alignment. A large portion of the exterior frame was top coated and other bare metal areas primed. Team Wylfa received an offer to re-metal the bogie wheel bearings from two members of the original No.134 team.

With both working NG/G16s back in service in May 2004, there was pressure to vacate the Goods Shed. The rolling chassis of the tender was mobile once more, leaving minor jobs such as refitting axlebox covers and fitting the drawbar, to allow the chassis to be shunted. Further stripping of the locomotive's chassis in late May and early June 2004 revealed the first unwelcome surprises: the rear frame stretcher was wasted to the point of reducing a ¾" thick web to a hole. This cast steel component also formed the pivot for the Bissel truck, and should be possible to repair by cropping out the corroded areas and welding in new plate. This severe corrosion had been the result of its position just beneath the front end of the firebox, where corrosive ash accumulations would be almost impossible to remove. Similarly, when the rear footplating was removed it revealed that the dragbox will need to be completely renewed, having also suffered heavy corrosion.

The project had now reached a critical point. To make further progress, the chassis would need to be lifted off the wheels so that the axleboxes and horn faces could be assessed and reconditioned. However, to do this the engine really needed to be under cover and, as ever, Dinas was severely restricted in rail connected covered accommodation. Any such accommodation was required for the operational railway. To have a long term project based in the loco shed, the goods shed or the carriage shed would have compromised the operation of daily services.

In mid 2004 the Clip Shed (built by the local authority in the 1950s and used by WHR volunteers for the restoration of second-hand South African rail fastenings – hence its name) was made available. This shed is situated at the north end of the yard, near

Left: *By November 2009 the frames had been de-scaled, cleaned and painted. One of the next tasks was to remove the rusted studs from the ends of the cylinder castings, visible in this photograph.* (Laurence Armstrong)

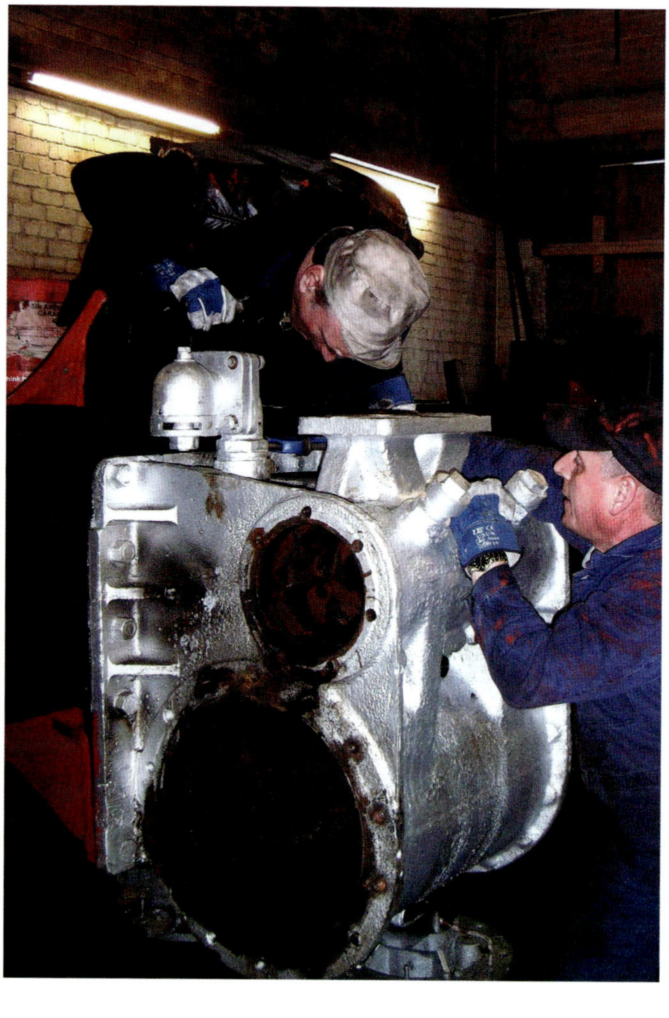

Below Left: *The removal of the cylinder end studs proved to be a struggle. This view shows the job well on the way to completion.* (Clive Briscoe)

the throat of the carriage shed. It is at right angles to the track, so laying new track would be necessary to run the loco into the building. Additionally, a crane would be needed to lift the loco off the rails and turn it through 90 degrees. By September of that year the shed was ready to receive the loco, but it was to be over a year, in October 2005, before a suitable crane was available at the right price. This occurred when a 100 tonne crane had some spare time on its way back to its depot from a job in Pwllheli. In the meantime, the clip shed had been prepared and the lighting and electrics improved such that the shed provided a suitable home for the restoration of a locomotive.

So, with No.134 moved into the shed and preparations complete, work could at last start in earnest on the chassis. But fate was about to intervene again. The management policy for motive power was still based around a homogeneous fleet of NG/G16s. Two were not going to be enough, with Nos.138 and 143 both approaching their 10-yearly overhaul dates. The spare NG/G16, No.140, was therefore moved from Glan-y-Pwll, where it had been stored since 1997, to Dinas. Team Wylfa was asked to help with its restoration so, once more, No.134 was relegated to the proverbial back-burner!

Those of us returning from South Africa in the spring of 2006 were inspired to get one of the NG15s back into traffic. We were convinced that not only could it hold its own against the NG/G16s in traffic, but that it would prove more efficient and easier to maintain. It was also clear that if the project was to succeed then it needed to be put on a firm project basis which would not be subject to the issues that had already brought the work to a halt several times. The Welsh Highland Railway Society was keen to see the loco restored – the then Chairman, Dave Kent, had been one of those on the trip to South Africa, along with both Tony Williams (Works Manager at Boston Lodge) and Jon Whalley (Chief Mechanical Engineer of the F&WHR). The Society was also looking for a new project to replace K1, as that loco was by then approaching its entry into service. Discussions commenced and showed that numerous issues needed to be resolved. Not the least were the rumours mentioned earlier about running downhill chimney first, running tender first, plus the appearance of the engine and whether we had the resources to do the work? The subsequent negotiations took two and a half years before the work could recommence. Eventually, however, they gave the sound footing on which we hope the loco will, at last, be completed.

Top: *The rear frame stretcher, which had been heavily corroded, had been refurbished and is seen here in January 2011, partially restored, being "dry-fitted" prior to re-attachment.* (Laurence Armstrong)

Centre top: *The fully refurbished stretcher and Bissell truck pivot is seen here being trial fitted in January 2012.* (Clive Briscoe)

Centre bottom: *A close-up view of the ribs of steel visible on the right hand side of the restored cast steel rear stretcher.* (Clive Briscoe)

Bottom: *By November 2011 progress had been made with forming the new running plate edging of the locomotive.* (Laurence Armstrong)

The basis of the agreement is as follows:

1. *The loco is and remains the property of the Festiniog Railway Trust.*
2. *The Society will fund all work being undertaken and return the completed locomotive to the Railway.*
3. *All work will be agreed with Boston Lodge before it is undertaken.*
4. *Wherever possible, Boston Lodge will be used to provide skilled labour and parts.*
5. *The Society will provide voluntary labour to carry out the assembly.*
6. *The loco is not being restored as a museumpiece but as a working steam engine, and modifications will therefore be made where appropriate to improve its performance on the WHR.*
7. *All modifications will be agreed with Boston Lodge before fitment to the loco.*
8. *All fundraising will be done so as not to interfere with that being carried out to complete the railway, e.g. the Phase 5 appeal.*

With the agreement in place, fundraising has been able to take place and a substantial fund built up to support the work of the group. Initial estimates were that £250k would be needed to complete the work. A contingency of a further £100k was added giving a target of £350k to be raised. An appeal to members over Christmas 2008 and the "Scrap to Steam" event in Caernarfon in August 2009 all boosted the bank balance. To date we have secured over 70% of the core money and we have a confident plan that will get us to completion in 2015. Our new campaign line is: "A 15 in 15."

The project was announced to the 2008 AGM of the WHRS and the first working party took place shortly afterwards on the weekend of 25th and 26th October. We were joined by Clive Briscoe from Team Wylfa, who remains a staunch member of the team. This continuity from the previous team was invaluable in finding out where component parts had got to and what was hidden where! Since then over thirty working parties have taken place and a significant amount of work has been completed. A group of over twenty working volunteers has been formed and we can regularly call on up to a dozen people for each working date.

The current status of the major components is as follows:

Boiler

The boiler currently stands outside the clip shed, sheeted and internally protected from the weather. A full ultrasonic test has been carried out and has not revealed too many issues. However, the bottom of the inner firebox will need replacement together with refitting of the foundation ring. This appears to be the fault that led to the engine being withdrawn, according to the note in the Driver's Log which the Society has in its care (the entry is in colloquial Afrikaans so the translation is challenging). The boiler will be repaired once the rest of the loco is virtually completed so that it does not have to be stored awaiting the completion of the engine.

Main Frames

The main frames have been completely stripped, sandblasted and painted. The corroded rear stretcher has been removed and repaired – at the end of 2011 it awaits machining so that it can be refitted. This will be challenging as the sides are at an angle. In the meantime the frames around it were also severely corroded and these have been built up with weld to return them to their original thickness. Once the stretcher is back in place the rear dragbox can be removed and replaced with a new one. The corrosion was too extensive to repair.

The axle alignment has been checked and datum set up so that the horns can be ground and axleboxes fitted. During this process it has been found that the cylinders are not a pair, one of them having been replaced during the loco's life. The right hand cylinder has also suffered from the liner being bored eccentrically. We will re-bore this to correct its alignment. Once these jobs are done then the reassembly of the chassis can commence.

Above: *On 29th April 2012 the Boston Lodge cylinder boring rig was busy with the refurbishment of the left hand cylinder of No.134 in the workshop at Dinas.* (Andie Shaw)

Cab & Superstructure

The cab structure will need complete replacement and will be rebuilt to match the lines of the new tender cab back. The opportunity will be taken to improve the cab design, the floor and sides being extended backwards to allow the cab access to be moved rearwards to be above the steps, rather than in front of them. Also the fall plates, located across the middle of the cab, will be moved to the rear, well away from standing areas. The brake shaft and reverser shaft have been removed for repair/ renewal. Both had suffered from some "agricultural" engineering during their working life with keyed joints replaced with blobs of weld!

Below: *This June 2011 view shows the eight wheelsets of the two tenders. The variety of their dissimilar sizes is apparent, as is the heavy wear of the far two sets.* (Terry Rowe)

Wheels

Boston Lodge has re-profiled all the loco wheels and they are ready to be re-assembled. The tender wheel sets have been held back. We intend to fit roller bearings under the tender (to avoid the regular maintenance task of oiling). When this is finally decided then the journals will need turning so that the jobs can be done together.

Boiler & Smokebox

The draughting arrangements will be reviewed to improve steaming. A Lempor exhaust is currently proposed but many other designs could be used – Kylchap, Giesel, or Lemaitre. All pipework and valves are missing so will need to be replaced. In the main the standard components used for the WHR NG/G16s will be used to allow interchangeability.

Left: *The new tender body for No.134 was delivered on 12th April 2012 from Brunswick Ironworks and mounted temporarily on the tender frames of No.133.* (Andie Shaw)

Tender Body

The tender bodies of both NG15s were in a poor state. By the summer of 2011 they had passed the stage where any recovery was possible and so were cut up leaving us with a spare, working chassis. For No.134 a completely new body was needed and, after much discussion, a design was arrived at and agreed. Brunswick Ironworks (another great local supporter of the railway) in Caernarfon was asked to build the new body. This matches the coal and water capacities of the NG/G16s, so that the operational range will be the same. The cab has a back for protection from the weather, the coal is now in a self trimming bunker and the lines of the loco have been carried across onto the tender so that the two will look as if they belong to each other.

Tender Chassis

Considerable corrosion has been found around the front dragbox, and the whole structure has been cut out to be replaced. As already mentioned the bogies are to be fitted with roller bearings. All of the brake gear and suspension needs re-bushing. While this is being done, a quick "wash and brush-up" has been done on No.133's frame, so that the new tender body is mobile and can travel about the railway.

In summary, we have not yet reached the point where the project is secure, but we are confident that in the next three to four years the loco will be completed. So far our cost estimates have been good and little recourse to the contingency has been necessary. This does not mean that we have all the funding – indeed a minimum of a further £70k will be needed to complete the project, quite possibly even £140k, but the team has plans in place to raise the money and a reasonable time to do it.

Sadly, project leader Peter Randall died in 2020, No. 134's restoration remaining incomplete. However, in 2018 the FR Company had sent its boiler to a contractor to be repaired and the locomotive's restoration is now moving along with the appointment of a new project leader.

- XIII -
Acknowledgements

The author thanks his many friends and colleagues on the F&WHR for their generous and valuable help, advice and information. Without it this book could not have been produced. Especial thanks go to Roy Woods (Editor, *The Snowdon Ranger* magazine) for his unstinting help and advice in the late stages of compiling the book. I thank Jon Whalley for his guidance and input. Thanks also go to Leith Paxton and Phil Girdlestone for the line drawings of the locomotives and for background information. A similar debt of gratitude is owed to Bruno Martin for his superb maps, some of which were created especially for this book. The chapters contributed by Peter Randall and John Hancock convey the feel of the different aspects of restoring and working on the trains on the WHR. I am also indebted to the late Dr Ben Fisher for the use of his excellent website, *www.whrsoc.org.uk/WHRProject/index.htm* for information on the re-building of Tasmanian Garratt K1.

I also gratefully thank the many photographers who have kindly allowed their work to be reproduced here. All the photographs are credited individually. Many of the images come, with permission from the Editor, from the file of photographs contributed by Society members to the Cymdeithas Rheilffordd Eryri (Welsh Highland Railway Society) magazine, *The Snowdon Ranger.* Others are from the F&WHR's official files on the company website. Records and photographs of our locomotives in their original working roles are surprisingly few and far between. It is a pleasure therefore to be able to thank Charlie Lewis, Peter Bagshawe, Gary Barnes, Neil Mardell, Phil Girdlestone, Tony Leeson, Robin Lake and Leith Paxton of South Africa for their help both with information and images. Especial thanks go to my many friends in the Apple Express Society in Port Elizabeth for their help with photos and information.

The summary of boiler information on South African Railway's overhauls was compiled by Mr Bob Bucher of Houston, Texas, who was a pioneer in the purchase and restoration of these classes of SAR locomotive. Archival photographic material collected by Terry Hutson in his former capacity as Editor of *SA Rail* is gratefully included, as are the information and photographs from Peter Ralph of the Puffing Billy Preservation Society, Melbourne.

The Crittenden Archive within the NGRS Library has been an invaluable source of historical information. I also thank Eric Conradie and Eurika Deminay of the (now closed) Transnet Heritage Library in Johannesburg for their help with SAR history. Completion of this book would have been impossible without their support. More locally an indispensable contribution has been made by Mr Dick Manton, also by Andrew Rutter of the K1 Group, the late Mr Neville Fields and the Archives of the Narrow Gauge Railway Society.

David Payling

- XIV -
Further Reading

There is unfortunately little literature devoted to the history of the narrow gauge Garratts and Kalaharis once to be seen running on South Africa's narrow gauge railways. A selection of references follow and it is hoped that this may lead readers to further rewarding information.

1. *24 Inches by SM Moir, Janus Publishing, 1981.*
2. *Namib Narrow Gauge by HT Crittenden and SM Moir, Janus Publishing, 1982.*
3. *German Colonial Railways Then and Now by H Schroeter and R Ramaer, Rohr Verlag, 1993.*
4. *The First 100 Years of State Railways in Namibia by B Bravenboer and WK Rusch, TransNamib Museum, 1997.*
5. *Garratt Locomotives of the World by AE Durrant, Bracken Books, 1987.*
6. *Beyer Peacock – Locomotive Builders to the World by RL Hills and D Patrick, Venture Publications, 1982.*
7. *Narrow Gauge Superpower by LD Paxton and DW Payling, The Narrow Gauge (No.192), 2006.*
8. *The NG/G16s by P Girdlestone and S McMahon, Railway World, November 1994, pp28-31.*
9. *Narrow Gauge Locomotives of South West Africa Part 1: Otavi Railway 0-6-2T and 2-8-2 Locomotives by LD Paxton and DW Payling, Continental Modeller, March 2009, pp138-142.*
10. *Narrow Gauge Locomotives of South West Africa Part 2: Otavi Railway Class He Pacifics by LD Paxton and DW Payling, Continental Modeller, April 2009, pp192-193.*
11. *Narrow Gauge Locomotives of South West Africa Part 3: Otavi Railway Class NG15 2-8-2 by LD Paxton and DW Payling, Continental Modeller, May 2009, pp278-283.*
12. *Gilding the Lily (SAR NG Locomotive Liveries) by R Manton and DW Payling, Continental Modeller, August 2010, pp42-499.*
13. *The Kalahari Story by DW Payling, Part 1, SA Rail, Oct-Dec 2002 (Vol.42, No. 3), and Part 2, SA Rail, Jan- Apr. 2003, Vol.42, No.4).*
14. *Henschel Locomotives for the South African Railways, Henschel Review, 11/1936, pp. 1 – 85.*
15. *Garratt Locomotives for South African Railways, Hanomag Nachrichten, Nov.- Dec. 1927, pp. 151 – 174.*
16. *Garratt Engines on South African Railways, South African Railways and Harbours Magazine, May 1928, 853.*
17. *Avontuur NG15 Class by I Jowett, Continental Modeller, Nov.-Dec. 1983, 218-220.*
18. *South African Narrow Gauge 2-8-2 Locomotives, The Locomotive, October 1953.*
19. *Here be Dragons A journey with steam to the end of the World by Phil Girdlestone, Camden Miniature Steam Services, 2017*
20. *The Railway to Adventure - a story of the 2 foot gauge railway from Port Elizabeth to Avontuur and Patensie by Charlie Lewis and David Payling, Ffestiniog Railway, 2020*

There are also various web sites where information can be found. A small selection follows:

Surviving Garratt Locomotives:
www.beyergarrattlocos.co.uk/survivors.html

Sandstone Heritage Trust:
www.sandstone-estates.com

Welsh Highland Railway Project:
www.whrsoc.org.uk/WHRProject/index.htm

- XV -
Appendices

1. *Dimensions of Selected Narrow Gauge Locomotives*

	Blanche	*Russell*	*Lyd*	*Merddin Emrys*	NG15	K1	NG/G13 & NG/G16
Builder	Hunslet	Hunslet	Boston Lodge	Boston Lodge	Various[1]	Beyer Peacock	Various[1]
Date Built	1893	1906	2010	1879	1931-1957[1.]	1909	1927-1968*
Wheel Arrangement	2-4-0TT	2-6-2T	2-6-2T	0-4+4-0T	2-8-2	0-4-0 + 0-4-0	2-6-2 + 2-6-2
Driving Wheel Diameter (in.)	26	28	33	32	33.875	31.5	33
Fixed Wheelbase (in.)	60	60	78	56	77.75	48	75
Boiler Pressure (p.s.i)	160	160	200	160	171	195	180
Cylinders (in.)	10.5 x 12	10.75 x 15	10.5 x 16	9 x 14	15.75 x 17.75	11 x 16 17 x 16	12 x 16
Tractive Effort (lb.) @ 85% BP	6920	8420	9087	9639	18893	14543	21360
Heating Surface (sq.ft.)	295	381	401	612[3.]	796	628	920
Superheater (sq. ft.)	44.25	21	30	42[3.]	21.6	None	147
Grate Area (sq. ft.)	5.2	6.25	8.74	12.4	16.7	14.8	19.2
Water Capacity (gall.)	270	440	550	667	2860	840	1825[2.]
Coal Capacity (ton)	Tender Oil Tank	0.725	(35 cu.ft.)	1 approx.	5.5	1.0	4.0[2.]
Wt in Working Order (tons)	15.3	20	25	24	67.75	33.5	60.6

1. *Various batches of these classes of locomotives were built between the dates shown (See Appendices 2 and 3).*
2. *The Tsumeb NG/G16s of 1958 carried 6.2 tons coal and 1325 gallons of water, being expected to run with a 3000 gallon tank car attached.*
3. Merddin Emrys *was built as a saturated engine locomotive. It was superheated when fitted with a new Hunslet boiler in the 1970s.*

BR STANDARD CLASSES*					
BR Standard Class	Wheel Arrangement	Grate Area Sq. Ft.	Weight in Working Order (t)	Wheel Diameter (in.)	Tractive Effort (85% BP)
4MT	2 – 6 – 4T	26.7	86.13	68	25515
3MT	2 – 6 – 2T	20.35	74	63	21490
2MT	2 – 6 – 2T	17.5	66.25	60	18513**
NG/G16	2 – 6 – 2+ 2 – 6 – 2	19.2	60.6	33	21360

* *Tank engine variant selected as the locomotive weight in working order includes the coal and water, as for the NG/G16s.*
** *Early examples of the similar Ivatt class 2MT 2-6-2T (1946) had smaller cylinders giving a Tractive Effort of 17410 lb.*

2. Dates and Details of the Final Boiler Overhaul of NG15 Locomotives by SAR Workshops

NG15 LOCOMOTIVES: SAR Overhaul Data, 1986							
Number	Builder	Loco. & Boiler Built	Works Number	First Boiler Carried	Last Major Overhaul by SAR	Current Boiler Carried	Current Boiler First Steamed
17	Henschel	1931	21905	8684	May 1976	10614	1953
18	Henschel	1931	21906	8685	July 1975	6999	1954
19	Henschel	1931	21907	8686	February 1983	7047	1957
117	Henschel	1938	24475	9323	October 1983	8686	1931
118	Henschel	1938	24476	9324	?	9324	1939
119	Henschel	1938	24477	9325	Sept. 1980/Feb. 1990	7045	1957
SPARE	Anglo-Franco-Belge	1950		6999			
120	Anglo-Franco-Belge	1950	2667	7008	November 1976	9323	1939
121	Anglo-Franco-Belge	1950	2668	7009	September 1976	10610	1953
122	Anglo-Franco-Belge	1950	2669	7010	March 1982	10613	1953
123	Anglo-Franco-Belge	1950	2670	7011	?	7010	1951
124	Anglo-Franco-Belge	1950	2671	7012	March 1986	7012	1951
132	Anglo-Franco-Belge	1953	2682	10610	July 1976	9325	1939
133	Anglo-Franco-Belge	1953	2683	10611	July 1979	8684	1931
134	Anglo-Franco-Belge	1953	2684	10612	September 1981	7043	1957
135	Anglo-Franco-Belge	1953	2685	10613	January 1979	7008	1951
136	Anglo-Franco-Belge	1953	2686	10614	December 1979	10611	1953
144	Henschel	1957	29585	7043	July 1977	7044	1957
145	Henschel	1957	29586	7044	Nov. 1980/ Oct. 1990	7009	1951
146	Henschel	1957	29587	7045	November 1981	10612	1953
147	Henschel	1957	29588	7046	July 1980	8685	1931
148	Henschel	1957	29589	7047	June 1982	7011	1951

Original Data collected by R Bucher, Houston, 1986. *Updated January 2004, RL Bucher and DW Payling.*

3. Dates and Details of the Final Boiler Overhaul of NG/G13 and NG/G16 Locomotives by SAR Workshops

Narrow Gauge Garratts: SAR Overhaul Data, 1986								
Class Steamed	Number	Builder	Loco. & Boiler Built	Works Number	First Boiler Carried	Last Major Overhaul by SAR	Current Boiler Carried	Current Boiler First Steamed
NG/G13	49	Hanomag	1928	10599	8306	March 1982	7019	1959
NG/G13	50	Hanomag	1928	10598	8307	January 1973	9067	1939
NG/G13	58	Hanomag	1927	10549	7850	September 1975	7852	1928
NG/G13	59	Hanomag	1927	10550	7851	1979	8306	1928
NG/G13	60	Hanomag	1927	10551	7852	November 1982	8784	1936
NG/G13	77	Hanomag	1928	10629	8384	August 1982	8786	1936
NG/G13	78	Hanomag	1928	10630	8385	September 1974	9063	1946
NG/G13	79	Hanomag	1928	10631	8386	April 1973	7015	1951
NG/G13	80	Hanomag	1928	10632	8387	May 1970	8388	1928
NG/G13	81	Hanomag	1928	10633	8388	October 1969	8385	1928
NG/G13	82	Hanomag	1928	10634	8389	?	8386	1928
NG/G13	83	Hanomag	1928	10635	8390	?	8389	1928
NG/G16	85	Cockerill	1936	3265	8784	September 1980	8785	1928
NG/G16	86	Cockerill	1936	3266	8785	November 1976	7018	1951
NG/G16	87	Cockerill	1936	3267	8786	August 1977	7850	1927
NG/G16	88	Cockerill	1936	3268	8787	July 1984	9060	1939
NG/G16	109	Beyer, Peacock	1939	6919	9060	April 1976	8387	1928
NG/G16	110	Beyer, Peacock	1939	6920	9061	August 1983	7036	1958
NG/G16	111	Beyer, Peacock	1939	6921	9062	December 1977	7020	1953
NG/G16	112	Beyer, Peacock	1939	6922	9063	September 1981	8307	1928
NG/G16	113	Beyer, Peacock	1939	6923	9064	March 1978	9065	1939
NG/G16	114	Beyer, Peacock	1939	6924	9065	June 1976	7038	1958
NG/G16	115	Beyer, Peacock	1939	6925	9066	April 1978	8384	1929
NG/G16	116	Beyer, Peacock	1939	6926	9067	October 1984	7851	1928

Narrow Gauge Garratts: SAR Overhaul Data, 1986 *(continued)*								
Class	Number	Builder	Loco. & Boiler Built	Works Number	First Boiler Carried	Last Major Overhaul by SAR	Current Boiler Carried	Current Boiler First Steamed
NG/G16	125	Beyer, Peacock	1950	7426	7013	October 1982	7035	1958
NG/G16	126	Beyer, Peacock	1950	7427	7014	August 1979	9064	1939
NG/G16	127	Beyer, Peacock	1950	7428	7015	October 1983	7013	1951
NG/G16	128	Beyer, Peacock	1950	7429	7016	July 1982	7042	1960
NG/G16	129	Beyer, Peacock	1950	7430	7017	June 1983	7111	1968
NG/G16	130	Beyer, Peacock	1950	7431	7018	February 1977	8787	1936
NG/G16	131	Beyer, Peacock	1950	7432	7019	September 1984	8390	1928
	SPARE	Beyer, Peacock	1950	-	7020			
NG/G16	137	Beyer, Peacock	1958	7862	7035	October 1981	7113	1968
NG/G16	138	Beyer, Peacock	1958	7863	7036	July 1981	7114	1968
NG/G16	139	Beyer, Peacock	1958	7864	7037	March 1983	7107	1968
NG/G16	140	Beyer, Peacock	1958	7865	7038	March 1984	9061	1939
NG/G16	141	Beyer, Peacock	1958	7866	7039	May 1981	7109	1968
NG/G16	142	Beyer, Peacock	1958	7867	7040	August 1978	7041	1958
NG/G16	143	Beyer, Peacock	1958	7868	7041	August 1977	7017	1951
	SPARE	Beyer, Peacock	1958	-	7042			
NG/G16	149	Hunslet Taylor	1967	3894	7106	June 1978	7014	1951
NG/G16	150	Hunslet Taylor	1967	3895	7107	October 1979	7112	1968
NG/G16	151	Hunslet Taylor	1968	3896	7108	October 1978	7037	1958
NG/G16	152	Hunslet Taylor	1968	3897	7109	June 1981	7106	1968
NG/G16	153	Hunslet Taylor	1968	3898	7110	June 1977	7040	1958
NG/G.16	154	Hunslet Taylor	1968	3899	7111	June 1982	7039	1958
NG/G16	155	Hunslet Taylor	1968	3900	7112	August 1980	7108	1968
NG/G16	156	Hunslet Taylor	1968	3901	7113	February 1981	7110	1968
	SPARE	Hunslet Taylor	1968	-	7114			

Original data collected by R Bucher, Houston, 1986. *Boiler identities checked by RL Bucher during South Africa visit in 2002, except for Nos. 110, 112.*

4. *Location of NG15 and NG/G13 and NG/G16 Locomotives*

The following lists give the location of the locomotives, updated to January 2022.

A) The NG15 Locomotives

17 Sandstone Railway, Ficksburg, SA (returned to service 07/2003)

18 Hempstead, Houston, Texas (Mr. R. Bucher)

19 Sandstone Railway, Ficksburg, SA (derelict condition)

117 Humewood Road Diesel Depot (stripped for parts, August 2011)

118 Bennett Brook Railway, Perth, Australia (currently under repair)

119 Apple Express (returned to service November 2008)

120 Surrey, UK (Rampton Collection, stored)

121 Surrey, UK (Rampton Collection, stored)

122 Railway Museum, George, SA

123 Bennett Brook Railway, Perth, Australia (back in service 2006)

124 Humewood Road running shed, (under restoration, 2010)

132 Scrapped at Humewood Road Diesel Depot, August 2011

133 WHR Dinas (awaiting overhaul)

134 WHR Dinas (under restoration, 2009)

135 Exmoor Steam Railway, UK (unrestored)

136 Sandstone Railway, Ficksburg, SA (2008)

144 Scrapped at Humewood Road Diesel Depot, August 2011

145 Scrapped at Humewood Road Diesel Depot, August 2011

146 Rampton Collection, UK, stored

147 Avontuur, SA (plinthed, in reasonably complete condition)

148 Scrapped at Humewood Road Diesel Depot, August 2011

B) The NG/G13 and NG/G16 Locomotives

49 Sandstone Railway, Ficksburg, SA, in service

50 Hempstead, Houston, Texas (Mr. R Bucher)

58 Sandstone Railway, Ficksburg, SA, unrestored

59 Scrapped after derailment and overturn, Pietermaritzburg, September 1982

60 Vale of Rheidol Railway, serviceable

77 Exmoor Steam Railway, partially restored

78 Germany, Private Owner, New Boiler 1997

79 Scrapped at Humewood Road Diesel Depot, August 2011

80 Joubertina Station, plinthed

81 Patensie Station, plinthed

82 Surrey, UK (Rampton Collection, stored)

83 Berlin Technical Museum, Germany

85 Sandstone Railway, Ficksburg, SA, unrestored

86 Sandstone Railway, Ficksburg, SA, unrestored

87 WHR, Dinas, in service

88 Sandstone Railway, Ficksburg, SA, serviceable 2010

109 Waterman Railway Heritage Trust, Peak Rail, Rowsley, Derbyshire, stored

110 Sandstone Estate, Ficksburg, unrestored

111 Gold Reef City

112 Century City, Cape Town (Loan from Sandstone)

113 Sandstone Railway, Ficksburg, SA, serviceable

114 Paddock, Natal, stored, Transnet Heritage Foundation

115 Exmoor Steam Railway, UK, stored

116 Paton Country NG Railway, Natal, long term restoration

125 Paddock, Natal, stored, Transnet Heritage Foundation

126 Paddock, Natal, stored, Transnet Heritage Foundation

127 Puffing Billy Preservation Society, Australia, 2012, in store

128 Sandstone Railway, Ficksburg, SA, unrestored

129 Puffing Billy Preservation Society, Australia, 1996, regauged and returned to steam 2019. Original boiler donated to WHR in 2014

130 WHR, Dinas, in service

131 Apple Express, Port Elizabeth, awaiting overhaul

137 Sandstone Railway, Ficksburg, SA, unrestored

138 WHR, Dinas, in service

139 Paddock, Natal, stored, Peter Newton

140 WHR, Dinas, awaiting overhaul

141 Sandstone Railway, Ficksburg, SA, unrestored

142 Paddock, Natal, stored, Peter Newton

143 WHR, Dinas, in service

149 Paddock, Natal, stored, Peter Newton

150 Sandstone Railway, Ficksburg, SA, unrestored

151 Paddock, Natal, stored, Peter Newton

152 Sandstone Railway, Ficksburg, SA, unrestored

153 Sandstone Railway, Ficksburg, SA, serviceable

154 Scrapped at Humewood Road Diesel Depot, August 2011

155 Sandstone Railway, Ficksburg, SA, unrestored

156 Paddock, Natal, stored, Peter Newton

- XVI -

Maps of the Narrow Gauge Railways in Southern Africa

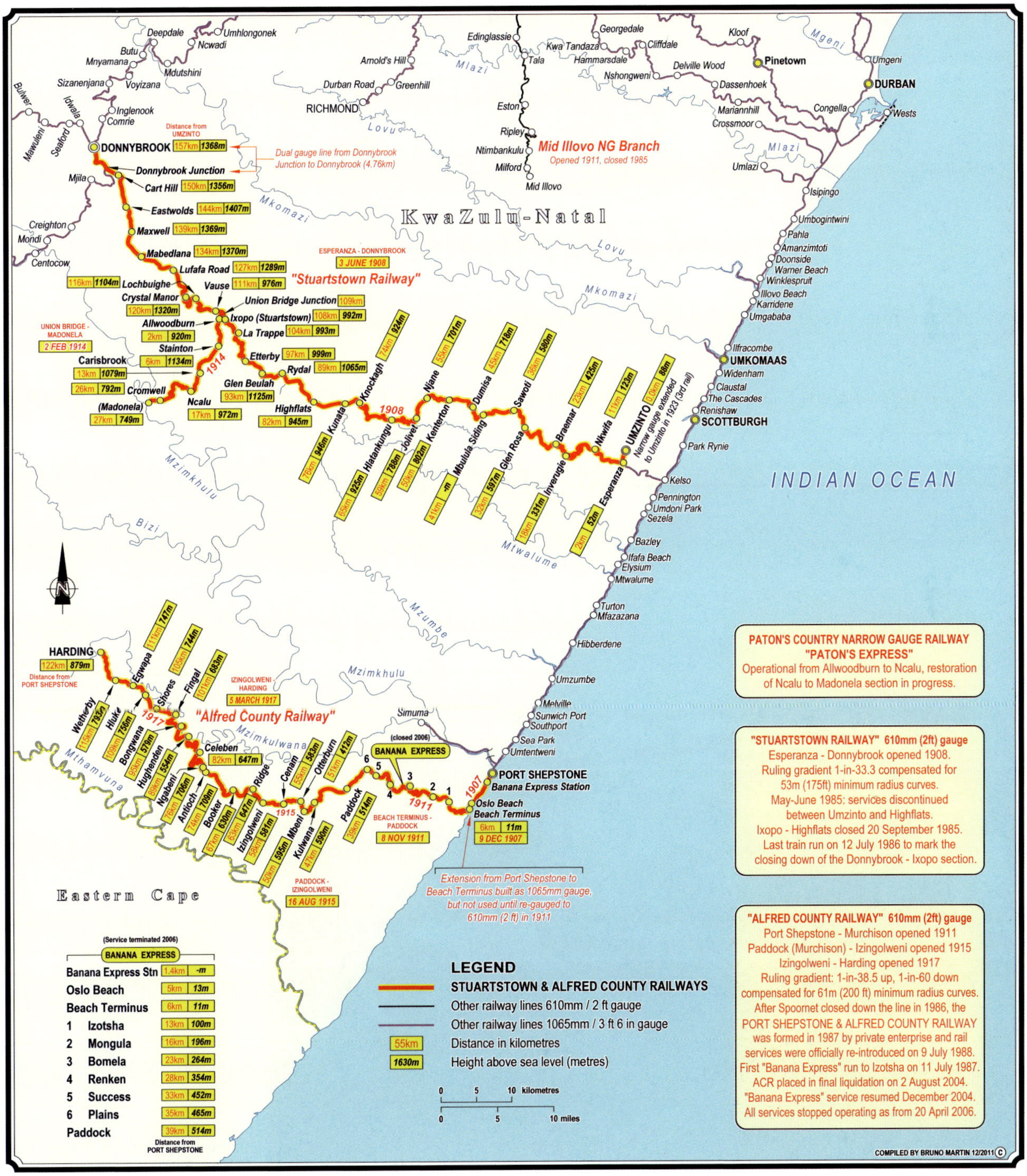

Cad file: DPaling-Natal-South-Coast.dwg

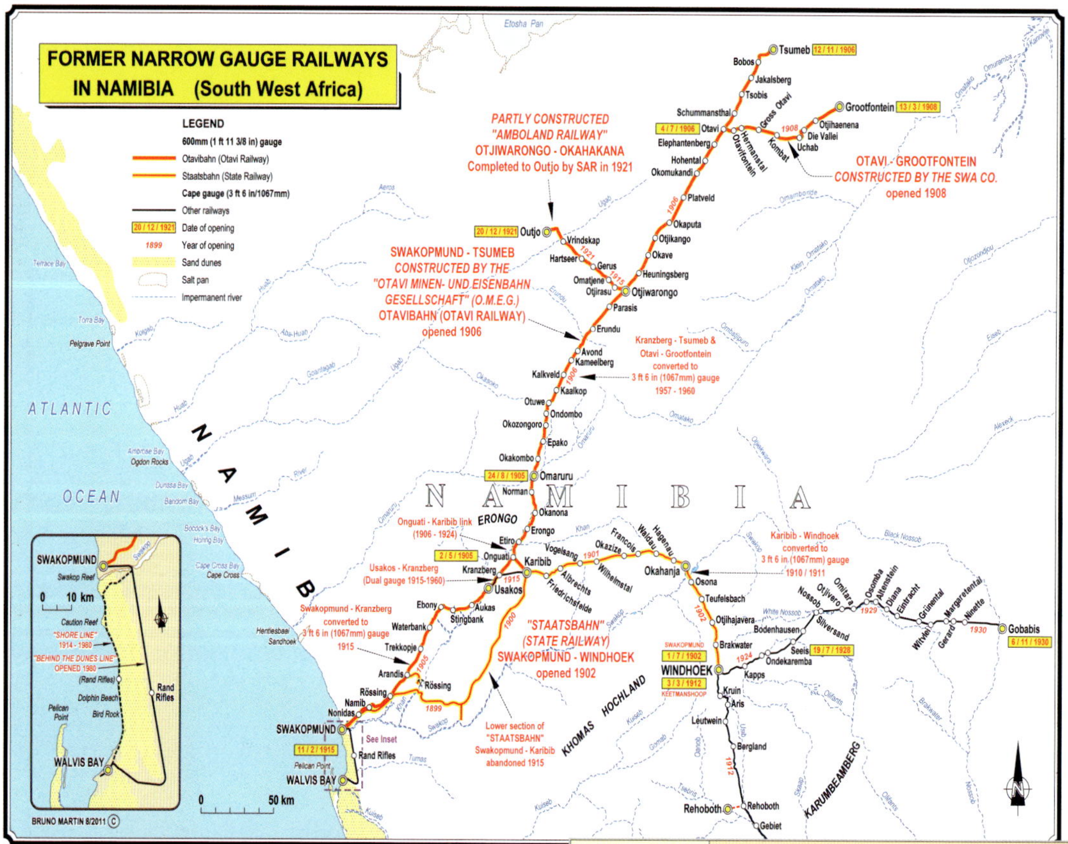

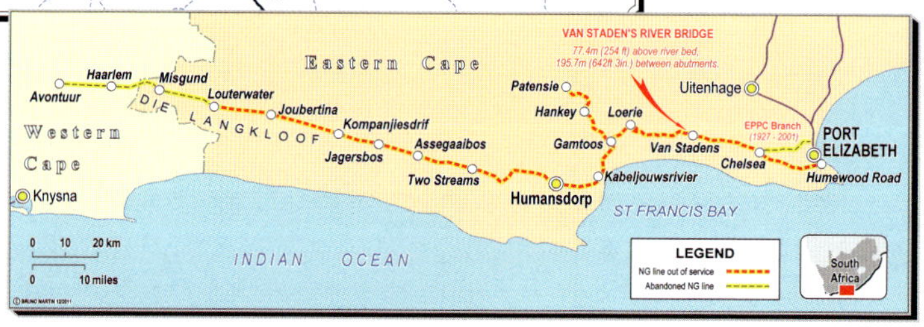

Left: *Following project leader Peter Randall's untimely death in 2020 Adrian Strachan took over the role, developing a plan to bring No. 134's restoration to a completion. He is seen (right) with the loco's frames in the loco shed at Dinas telling a group of supporters about his plans in September 2021.* (Peter Johnson)

- XVII -

Drawings

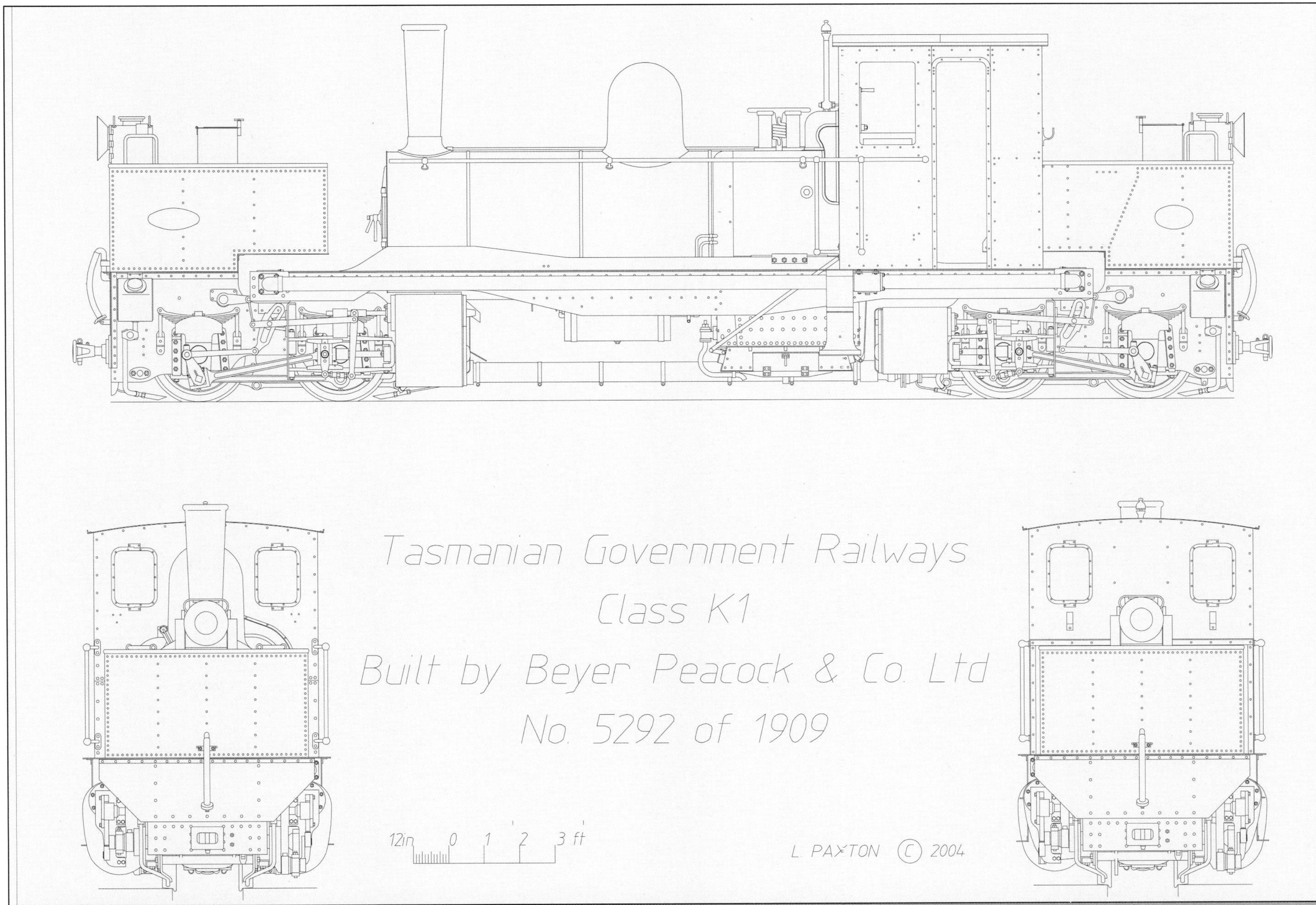

NG/G16 (Phil Girdlestone)

- XVIII -
NG/G13s in the UK

Two of the NG/G13 forerunners are preserved in the UK. No 77 **(above)** *was imported for the Brecon Mountain Railway in 1986 and was photographed there soon after arrival. It was sold to the Exmoor Steam Railway in 2003 and remains there.* (Peter Johnson collection)

No 60 **(right)** *was purchased by a group of Swiss enthusiasts, also in 1986, and restored to working order in 1998, running on the Schinznacher Baumschulbahn for several years. Since 2017 it has been based at the Vale of Rheidol Railway, where it was commissioned early in 2022. It was photographed at Aberystwyth on 11 June 2018.* (Peter Johnson)

Index